The English Heritage
Baking
Book

 **English Heritage**

Heritage is for everybody. That's why, as a charity, English Heritage cares for over a million objects and hundreds of historic sites in every part of England, from international icons to local treasures. And it's why they open them up, share their stories and find new ways for everybody to enjoy, learn, play and create. By buying this book, you're helping the charity to be there for heritage.

The English Heritage
Baking
Book

A timeless collection of recipes
inspired by England's history

First published in Great Britain in 2025 by Seven Dials,
an imprint of The Orion Publishing Group Ltd
Carmelite House, 50 Victoria Embankment
London EC4Y 0DZ

An Hachette UK Company

The authorised representative in the EEA is Hachette Ireland,
8 Castlecourt Centre, Dublin 15, D15 XTP3, Ireland (email: info@hbgi.ie)

10 9 8 7 6 5 4 3 2 1

A CIP catalogue record for this book is
available from the British Library.

ISBN (Hardback) 978 1 3996 2942 3
ISBN (Ebook) 978 1 3996 2943 0

Printed in Italy by by Printer Trento

MIX
Paper | Supporting
responsible forestry
FSC
www.fsc.org   **FSC® C104740**

www.orionbooks.co.uk

Contents

Introduction

Introduction

There is no denying that, as a nation, we have a sweet tooth. Walk down any high street today and bakeries still display a range of treats designed to tempt us inside.

The smell of butter, sugar and flour drifts on the wind in our cities – pumped into supermarket car parks – because nothing is so comforting or seductive as the smell of freshly baked bread. And yet we seem to have been persuaded to abandon our baking heritage in recent decades.

Some British classics persist – the Eccles cake (see page 14) is still found widely in various forms, but others, such as the pound cake and bara brith (see pages 36 and 98) have all but disappeared. Travel widely with a keen eye, and you will find them tucked away in small high-street bakeries, holding out against competition from supermarkets churning out American muffins and cupcakes in astonishing variety.

Whatever you bake, your results will only be as good as the ingredients you use, so aim to use high quality, responsibly sourced ingredients. If you only allow yourself one piece of cake a week, you will want to make sure it is a very good piece of cake, and homemade cake is always best.

Techniques

Creaming

The butter in cakes, such as the Victoria sandwich cake, is creamed. Here, softened, room-temperature butter is beaten with a wooden spoon or large whisk to add air. This lightens the butter's texture and colour. Once the butter has been beaten, sugar is added and the mixture beaten again, further lightening the mixture. Finally, egg is gradually beaten in resulting in a mixture that is shiny and glossy.

The main aim in creaming a mixture is to add the egg gradually and to beat the mixture thoroughly between each addition. This allows the egg and butter to be emulsified together properly, resulting in a mixture that holds air. If this emulsified mixture is broken, or curdled, a portion of the air is lost and the mixture will be heavier.

Whisking

This is the action of adding air to a mixture to lighten it in colour and texture. A metal balloon whisk is the best tool – either hand held or machine driven. Ingredients that are commonly whisked include eggs and cream. Properly whisked egg whites go through a dramatic transformation, first becoming frothy, and then turning pure white with a light and fluffy texture rather like shaving foam. The mixture should be able to hold its shape rather than run back into the bowl. In some recipes egg whites are whisked on their own before being folded into the other ingredients; in others (for example when making meringues), they are whisked with sugar, which gives them a glossier appearance and a firmer set. A meringue mixture is often said to be able to hold 'stiff peaks'. Egg yolks, when whisked, will pale significantly in colour and increase in volume, but they will never hold their shape as firmly as egg whites.

Folding

The aim when folding two or more ingredients together is to limit the loss of air from the mixture, and this is a method used commonly in baking and dessert cookery. The best tool to use is a large metal spoon or spatula, using a gentle motion of folding one ingredient into the other to blend them – as opposed to beating them – together.

Kneading

The technique of mixing and working dough, usually made of flour, yeast and water, in order to make it into a cohesive, supple mass, is known as kneading. This can be done either by hand or using a machine. However, once you have brought the ingredients together with your hands to make the dough, you should leave it to rest for 20 minutes before kneading.

Kneading plain, white bread-flour dough
Place the rested dough on a lightly floured work surface, and flour your hands. Using one hand to anchor the dough in front of you, push the heel of your other hand into the dough, stretching it as you push it away from you. Use your fingertips to pull the leading edge of the dough back over the middle portion, forming a ball, and repeat this action.

As you knead, occasionally take a piece of dough the size of a golf ball and stretch it between the first and second fingers of both hands. The aim is to make a thin window-like sheet of dough that stretches without tearing until it is thin enough to see light through. You will notice that as you knead this becomes increasingly possible, and this is a sign that the dough is developing. If the dough tears when stretched, keep kneading.

Kneading wholemeal bread-flour dough

Because wholemeal flour contains small pieces of wheat bran, it requires slightly different handling to white flour. It is even more important to leave the freshly mixed dough to rest before kneading for it to be able to develop properly. Knead the dough in stages, allowing it to rest for a couple of minutes occasionally before kneading it again. Do this over a period of 10–15 minutes.

When the dough (either plain white or wholemeal) is shiny and resistant but still very slightly sticky, it is fully developed. Now it can be left to rise in a large bowl in a warm place, covered with either a damp tea towel or oiled cling film.

Making yeast sponges for richer doughs

Bakers occasionally start a batch of yeasted dough using what is known as a 'sponge'. This is a loose batter made from a portion of the liquid, yeast and flour to be used in a recipe which will both give a deeper flavour and, especially when using spices, eggs or fat, a lighter texture because these ingredients tend to inhibit the action of the yeast.

Cooking techniques

Temperature and timing

The high sugar content of baked goods means that they are prone to overcooking if the oven heat is too fierce. Fan ovens (also called convection ovens) circulate hot air in the oven and so reduce cooking times. The timings in this section have been worked out using a fan oven. If yours is a conventional oven, raise the heat given in the recipes by 10°C, and expect the recipes to take slightly longer.

Where you place a tray of biscuits or a cake in the oven will affect how they bake, especially if you have a conventional oven. Place them too close to one side of the oven and they will cook unevenly. Because of this, it is wise to turn cakes and biscuits when they begin to brown so that they colour and rise evenly.

Steam

Bread benefits from being baked in a humid, steamy environment. Steam slows down the formation of the crust, allowing the bread to rise more, producing a lighter loaf. You can introduce steam to the oven by placing a small roasting tin on the bottom of the oven when you first turn the oven on to preheat. Then add hot water to the tin just after you put the bread in. Be careful not to scald yourself with the steam, as it will rise violently when you pour the water in.

Lining cake tins

Cake or loaf tins are generally greased and lined before baking, even if they are non-stick. As well as making it easier to remove the finished cake or loaf from the tin, lining with baking paper makes tins easier to clean. Use melted butter, brushed into all the corners and edges of the tin, and then cut non-stick baking paper to fit. This paper is coated to prevent sticking – and is especially good when used with meringues, which tend to stick to aluminium foil or greaseproof paper.

Testing whether cakes and breads are cooked

To test whether a cake is cooked, insert a skewer into the centre and remove it. If it comes away clean, the cake is cooked. This method will not work for cakes that are intentionally left slightly undercooked for a fudgy effect, such as the dark chocolate cake on page 74.

To test whether a bread is cooked, slip it from its tin and tap the bottom gently with your knuckles. If the bread gives a hollow sound, it is cooked.

Alternatively, a temperature probe can be inserted into cakes and breads once they have reached the end of their cooking time. If a temperature of 95°C has been reached at the centre, the cake or bread is cooked.

Storing baked goods

Always store cakes and biscuits in airtight containers to stop them becoming stale. Butter-based cakes and biscuits keep very well, but they do eventually grow stale if not eaten. In the event that you end up with some stale cake, you can use it up in a queen's pudding (see page 46).

Bread goes stale quickly. Even the act of freezing bread seems to hurry it past its best. To extend its keeping time, wrap it well in a cloth bag and store it in a cool place.

Puddings and cold desserts

From the lightest lemon posset to a luscious trifle with its complex layering, puddings are a delicious way to end a meal. They should strike a balance between sheer decadence and perfect good taste, and each should fit its occasion. Choose a pudding well, and make it expertly, and your meals will be legendary among your friends and family.

Cold puddings

A chilled dessert is lovely at the end of a summer lunch or dinner, and because the British summer provides us with such lovely berries, one need look no further than a posset or cremet, or perhaps a custard to accompany macerated strawberries or raspberries (served at room temperature for the best flavour). Fruit jellies offer an excellent, light-handed way of making vibrantly fresh desserts to round off a rich meal. The one given here, for strawberry jelly (see page 126) will be a revelation to anyone who makes it.

Of course, cold puddings are not limited only to the months of summer. Poached autumn fruits, such as pears, or winter fruits, such as rhubarb, make delicious accompaniments to a serving of homemade cream cheese. Seville oranges are a truly seasonal fruit, and only available in the depths of winter. But don't just save them for marmalade. The zest is delicious and can be used to scent custards wonderfully.

For an added indulgence, cold puddings are delicious served with a homemade biscuit or two.

Hot puddings

On a cold day, the rich, seductive aroma of a chocolate soufflé (see page 122) or the nutmeg-scented fragrance of a rice pudding (see page 112) heralds the arrival of perfect comfort food.

Traditional hot puddings are usually mixtures of flour, suet and fruit that have been bound together in a cloth and then boiled or

steamed. However, there are other traditional hot puddings, such as
Bakewell Pudding (see page 22), which are set in pastry cases and
baked rather than steamed. Serve this hot pudding in a warmed bowl,
preferably with Jersey cream or custard (see page 116).

Fruit puddings

Fruit is an incredibly versatile ingredient, and is widely used in
puddings and desserts. In addition, many simple creams and custards
are delicious served with fresh or poached fruit alongside. Choose
whatever is in season, and cook it lightly with a little sugar and lemon
or orange juice.

Chocolate

Plain chocolate with a high percentage of cocoa (usually more than
60%) is the best type of chocolate for cooking with. As the percentage
of cocoa increases, the percentage of other ingredients, mostly sugar,
decreases. Professional cooking chocolate or couverture is 'tempered',
a process involving heating and cooling it under certain conditions.
The result is a chocolate that breaks cleanly and melts sublimely. Milk
chocolate contains a high proportion of milk solids and, consequently,
has a lower cocoa content. White chocolate contains only cocoa
butter from the cocoa beans, and has no cocoa mass at all.

Always melt chocolate slowly. All forms of chocolate should be
kept in a cool dark environment, and it is best to only buy what you
need, as chocolate stales quickly.

A note on gelatine

Gelatine, which is derived from cartilage-rich animal tissues and bones, is the most commonly used setting agent in the kitchen today. Historically, other substances have been used as setting agents, including carageen moss (a seaweed), isinglass (derived from the swim bladders of fish) and agar agar (another seaweed derivative).

Gelatine can be bought in powdered form, but clear, brittle sheet gelatine has a finer flavour, gives a more accurate result and is easier to measure. In the course of testing the recipes for this book, we tested all of the different types of gelatine available. Platinum grade sheets weighing approximately 1.6g each are the best type, and are easy to obtain. Three sheets of this gelatine are sufficient to give a light set to 500ml of jelly served in a glass. If you want to use a mould and will need to turn the jelly out, use four sheets per 500ml.

To use leaf gelatine

Cover sheets of leaf gelatine in cold water for a minimum of 10 minutes to soften them. Give them a squeeze and then add them to the warm liquid that is specified in the particular recipe you are following, stirring to dissolve them. They will not dissolve if the water is cold.

Vegetarian gelatine can be bought, but will set while still quite warm, making it difficult to use with cold mousses (because it needs to be used warm, which tends to melt the cream when mixed). It is suitable for fruit jellies, however. Simply follow the manufacturer's instructions.

Pastry
& Buns

Flaky Shortcrust Pastry

 **MAKES ENOUGH FOR I X 22–25CM PIE**

Preparation time 10 minutes plus 1 hour chilling time

250g plain flour

pinch salt

150g cold unsalted butter

½ tsp lemon juice

100ml iced water

If you have a food processor, sift the flour and salt into the bowl and mix. Cut 100g of the butter into rough cubes and add them to the flour mixture. Pulse until it resembles fine breadcrumbs. Cut the rest of the butter into small cubes, add them the blender and pulse briefly to combine. Small lumps of butter should still be obvious in the mixture.

If you are working by hand, sift the flour and salt into a large bowl. Coarsely grate 100g of the butter into the flour mixture. Rub the butter and flour between your fingertips working quickly to keep the mixture as cool as possible. If it starts to feel sticky, chill the mixture for 30 minutes. Then coarsely grate the remaining butter into the mixture and stir. Small lumps or strands of butter should be clearly visible.

Chill the mixture for 30 minutes. Just before you are ready to proceed, stir the lemon juice into the water and pour two-thirds of this into the flour mixture. Blend well with a fork. Using your fingertips, bring the dough together, adding more water as necessary until everything is evenly mixed and there are no dry lumps of flour. Bring the mixture together into a smooth lump, carefully form it into a ball, wrap in cling film and chill for at least 1 hour before using.

Sweet Pastry

 **MAKES APPROX 700G**

🕐 *Preparation time 10 minutes plus 1–2 hours chilling time*

The key here is to blend the butter with the flour and, to make this easier, you start off with butter at room temperature, and then beat it until it is light, as you would if you were making a cake. The pastry is then chilled before use, and kneaded lightly to make it supple before rolling it out. This pastry recipe makes enough for a 30cm tart case.

200g unsalted butter, at room temperature

125g icing sugar

1 medium egg, lightly beaten

285g plain flour, plus extra for dusting

In a large bowl, cream the softened butter with a wooden spoon until light. Sift in the icing sugar and combine gently until well mixed.

Add the beaten egg to the bowl, mixing well, then sift in the flour and combine well. When you have obtained a soft dough scrape it into a ball and then flatten it onto a piece of cling film. Cover the dough with the cling film and chill.

After 1–2 hours the dough will be easier to handle. When you are ready to roll out the pastry, remove it from the cling film and knead it lightly to make it supple enough for rolling. Place a sheet of non-stick baking paper on your work surface and scatter it with a little flour. Place the dough on the baking paper and cover with another sheet of baking paper, then roll out between the 2 sheets.

Shortcrust Pastry

Preparation time 10 minutes plus 1 hour chilling time

250g plain flour

pinch salt

125g cold unsalted butter, cubed or grated

½ tsp lemon juice

100ml iced water

If you have a food processor, sift the flour and salt into the bowl and mix. Add the cubed or grated butter and pulse until the mixture resembles fine breadcrumbs. Pour the mixture into a bowl.

If you are working by hand, sift the flour and salt into a bowl and add the cubed or grated butter. Rub the butter and flour between your fingertips until it resembles fine breadcrumbs, working quickly to keep the mixture as cool as possible. If it starts to feel sticky, chill the mixture for 30 minutes before moving on to the next step.

Add the lemon juice to the water and pour two-thirds of this into the flour mixture. Blend well with a fork, stirring quickly but gently. Using your fingertips, bring the dough together. Add more water as necessary (you may need to use all of it) until everything is evenly mixed and there are no dry lumps of flour. Bring the mixture together into a smooth, supple lump. Carefully form the pastry into a flattened ball, wrap in cling film and chill for at least 1 hour before using.

Suet Pastry

 **MAKES APPROX 600G**

Preparation time 10 minutes plus 30 minutes chilling time

375g self-raising flour	130g suet, grated
scant 1 tsp salt	250ml cold water

Sift the flour and salt into a large bowl and mix in the suet. Add half of the water. Stir well with a fork, working quickly but gently. Using your fingertips, bring the dough together. Add more water as necessary until everything is evenly mixed and there are no dry lumps of flour.

Bring the mixture together into a smooth, supple lump. Carefully form it into a ball, wrap in cling film and chill for 30 minutes before using.

Puff Pastry

 MAKES 2KG

*⏱ Preparation time 15 minutes
plus 20 minutes of rolling over 3 hours*

1kg strong plain flour, plus
extra for dusting

2 tsp salt

1kg cold unsalted butter

1 tsp lemon juice

500ml cold water

Using a food processor, place all the flour with the salt and 250g of the butter, cut into cubes, into the bowl and pulse until the mixture resembles fine breadcrumbs. Pour this into a large bowl.

Add the lemon juice to the water and add two-thirds of the liquid to the bowl. Blend well with a fork, stirring quickly but gently. Using your fingertips, bring the dough together. Add more water as necessary (you may need all of it) until everything is evenly mixed and there are no dry lumps of flour. Bring the mixture together into a smooth, supple lump. Carefully form it into a flattened ball, wrap in cling film and chill for at least 1 hour before using.

Roll the remaining butter between 2 sheets of non-stick baking paper into an 18cm square that is 2.5cm thick. Lightly flour your work surface, then remove the dough from the fridge and unwrap. Place on the lightly floured surface and cut a deep cross in the dough, cutting about two-thirds of the way through to the work surface. Dust the ball with flour and fold the 4 segments out into a rough square shape.

Dust this lightly with flour and roll it into a square about 28cm across, or large enough to take the block of butter set at a 45° angle.

Using a clean pastry brush, dust the pastry free of flour, place the butter in the centre at a 45° angle to the pastry and fold each corner of the pastry over the butter, pinching the dough together to seal any holes. Turn the dough over, dusting the work surface again with a little flour, and roll the pastry out into a 20 x 60cm rectangle. If the pastry sticks to the work surface dust it with a little more flour as required.

Once you have a rectangle of the right size, brush the pastry to remove any excess flour. Fold the third of the pastry nearest to you over the middle third, then fold in the top third on top of that so that you have a 20 x 20cm square and press, keeping the dough as square and even as you can. Place it on a plate in a cool place or the fridge to rest.

After 15 minutes remove the dough from the fridge and turn it 90° to the right from its original position, so that the top open fold is on your left. Roll out again to 20 x 60cm and repeat the action above. Do this a total of 6 times, allowing the dough to rest in between each fold. After resting it for the last time, roll the pastry into a 30 x 20cm rectangle. Cut this evenly into 4 parts. If you are not using any of the puff pastry straight away, wrap each portion tightly in cling film, then seal in foil and freeze.

Enriched Dough for Sweet Buns

🕐 *Preparation time 20 minutes plus 1–1¼ hours rising and resting time*

Historically, yeasted sweet cakes were far more common than they are now – we tend to use eggs to leaven cakes today, as they are widely available year round (which they weren't historically) and relatively inexpensive. The recipes that use this dough often have a very regional basis, but they can all be made from the same basic dough, with only minor adjustments. The basic dough recipe is given here.

80ml water

75ml whole milk

5g dried yeast

220g strong white flour

2 egg yolks

55g plain white flour, plus extra for dusting

¾ tsp salt

30g caster sugar

30g butter, melted

SPECIAL EQUIPMENT:

a temperature probe

First, heat the water and milk in a small saucepan over a low heat until the mixture is tepid, not more than 30°C.

In a large bowl, whisk this mixture with the yeast and 130g of the strong flour until the ingredients combine into a smooth batter. Cover and leave in a warm place for 45 minutes to an hour, or until doubled in size.

Beat the egg yolks into the batter then combine the flour, salt and sugar together and add to the batter. Use your hands to bring all the ingredients together and knead for 2 minutes.

Next add the melted butter a little at a time and continue to mix until all the butter is incorporated. Rest the dough, covered with a damp tea towel, in a warm place for 15 minutes then proceed as advised for each recipe.

Lemon Tart

 SERVES 8

Preparation time 30 minutes plus 30 minutes resting time

Cooking time 1 hour 15 minutes

Lemons have always been a popular dessert ingredient, providing a refreshing counterbalance to a rich meal. This classic tart is a perfect example, with the almonds adding a pleasant texture to the zesty filling. The original recipe uses a puff pastry case, but the shortcrust gives a weightier, more refined edge.

½ quantity shortcrust pastry (see page 4)

150g caster sugar

90ml double cream

6 egg yolks

150g butter, melted

40g ground almonds

zest and juice of 2 large lemons

SPECIAL EQUIPMENT:

a 22cm metal pie or baking dish

some baking beans

First make the pastry and leave it to rest in the fridge for 20 minutes. Then, roll it out on a floured surface to a 27cm round. Place it in the pie dish, leaving the extra pastry hanging over the edge. This technique may seem wasteful, but it will help prevent the pastry shrinking back into the case.

Line the pastry case with a large piece of non-stick baking paper and then fill with baking beans. Leave to rest in a cool place for 10 minutes.

Preheat the oven to 200°C/gas mark 7. Place the pastry case on a baking tray and bake for 35 minutes until the pastry is firm and golden brown. Remove the beans and paper and return the case to the oven for five minutes to bake further and dry slightly.

Remove from the oven and set aside. Reduce the oven to 120°C/gas mark 1.

Now make the filling by beating together the sugar and cream. Then beat in the egg yolks. Beat the melted butter into the mixture, adding it a little at a time.

Fold in the ground almonds along with the lemon juice and zest. Pour the mixture into the pastry case and bake for 40 minutes, or until just set.

Trim the pastry hanging over the rim with a sharp knife and cool to room temperature before serving.

Steamed Blackcurrant Pudding

 SERVES 6

🕐 *Preparation time 20 minutes plus 10 minutes resting time*

🍳 *Cooking time 3 hours*

This recipe for a blackcurrant, or gooseberry, pudding steamed in a suet crust may sound formidable, but this is a splendid thing – steaming, vivid purple with the juice from the fruits, and with an intensity of flavour you will rarely find.

---

butter, for greasing

1½ quantities suet pastry
(see page 5)

FOR THE FILLING:

400g fresh or frozen

blackcurrants, picked weight

150g caster sugar

SPECIAL EQUIPMENT:

a 2-litre pudding basin

pastry cutter or muffin ring

Grease the pudding basin and set aside. Make the suet pastry and leave it to rest for 10 minutes. Roll out two-thirds of the pastry and use it to line the pudding basin. Roll out the remainder to make the lid.

Thoroughly combine the fruit and sugar in a bowl. Transfer the mixture into the dough-lined pudding basin. Wet the top edge of the pastry, and place the lid on. Gently seal the edges and trim off any excess.

Take a large piece of greaseproof paper and pleat it down the centre to allow room for expansion during steaming. Cover the top of the pudding with this and then a pleated layer of foil and secure with kitchen string around the edge of the basin, leaving some extra string to make a handle for lifting the pudding basin.

Fill the kettle with water and bring to the boil. Place a pastry cutter or muffin ring in the bottom of a 4-litre pan and set it on the hob. Set the pudding basin on the ring in the bottom of the pan (this ensures that the basin does not crack) and add boiling water to a depth of 15cm. Turn the heat under the pan to medium and bring the water to a simmer. Continue simmering over a low heat for 3 hours, topping up with boiling water as necessary.

After 3 hours, lift the pudding basin out of the pot and remove the paper and foil lid. Turn the pudding out of the basin onto a serving dish. Serve with custard (see pages 116) or Jersey cream.

Eccles Cakes

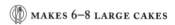 **MAKES 6–8 LARGE CAKES**

🕐 *Preparation time 10 minutes*   🍳 *Cooking time 35 minutes*

Some historical recipes for mince pies were made with puff pastry rather than the shortcrust that is more often used today, giving a result that is strongly reminiscent of Eccles cakes. Here, the mincemeat filling has been replaced with a simple mixture of currants and lemon zest to create a true Eccles cake. These are delicious served with some good Cheshire or Lancashire cheese. If you've got some homemade puff pastry (see page 6) in the freezer, thaw out 500g and use it here.

500g currants

125g unsalted butter

125g caster sugar, plus an extra pinch

zest of 2 lemons

plain flour, for dusting

500g puff pastry (see pages 6–7)

1 egg white, beaten

pinch caster sugar

granulated sugar, for dredging

SPECIAL EQUIPMENT:

a 10–12cm round pastry cutter

Preheat the oven to 200°C/gas mark 7 and line a baking sheet with non-stick baking paper. Place the currants, butter, caster sugar and lemon zest in a small pan over a low heat. Cook, stirring, for 5 minutes then remove from the heat and leave to cool.

Scatter some flour onto your work surface and roll the puff pastry out to a 3–4mm thick sheet. Cut out 6–8 rounds using a cutter (or a small saucer). Re-roll any trimmings if you need to.

Divide the filling between the circles and dampen the edges of the pastry with a little water. Bring the edges together, making sure the filling is covered, and pinch hard, twisting off any excess. Turn the balls over, flattening them slightly, keeping their shape circular. Place on the prepared baking sheet.

Mix the beaten egg white with a pinch of caster sugar and brush the mixture over the cakes, then sprinkle them heavily with granulated sugar. Finally, cut a 2cm slit in the top of each.

Bake for 20 minutes, or until the cakes are brown and crispy then turn the heat down to 140°C/gas mark 3 for a further 15 minutes. The cakes are ready when the undersides are browned and firm. Remove to a cooling rack.

Once the cakes are completely cold, they can be stored in an airtight tin for up to 3 days.

Treacle Tart

🕐 *Preparation time 20 minutes*

🍳 *Cooking time 30 minutes*

Treacle Tart is a classic British dessert with roots in the late 19th century, when golden syrup – confusingly called "light treacle" – became a kitchen staple. Originally a thrifty recipe using breadcrumbs, syrup and lemon in a shortcrust pastry, it quickly became a comforting favourite across Britain. Sweet, sticky and warmly nostalgic, it's been a staple at Sunday dinners and even found fame as Harry Potter's favourite dessert. Despite its humble beginnings, Treacle Tart remains a beloved treat, celebrated for its balance of rich syrup and bright citrus.

45ml/3 tbsp golden syrup
50g soft white breadcrumbs
1 tsp lemon juice
1 quantity of short crust pastry (see page 4)
150g plain flour

½ tsp salt
65g margarine
flour, for dusting

SPECIAL EQUIPMENT:
a 20cm pie plate

Preheat the oven to 200°C/gas mark 6. To make the pastry, sift the flour and salt in a bowl, then rub in the margarine until the mixture resembles fine breadcrumbs. Add enough cold water to make a stiff dough. Press the dough together with your fingertips.

Roll out the pastry on a lightly floured surface and use just over three-quarters of it to line a 20cm pie plate, reserving the rest for a lattice topping.

Melt the syrup in a saucepan. Stir in the breadcrumbs and lemon juice, then pour the mixture into the prepared pastry case.

Roll out the reserved pastry to a rectangle and cut into 1cm strips. Arrange in a lattice on top of the tart. Bake for about 30 minutes.

A Brief History of
THE BRITISH
MINCE PIE

The British mince pie can be traced back to medieval recipes containing a mixture of meat, fruit, suet, and spices. During that time, it was common to mix sweet and savoury flavours in meat dishes. A collection of recipes from the 14th century, known as *Forme of Cury*, contains a recipe for a sweetened, meaty version of a pie. The list of extravagant ingredients includes minced pork, cheese, lard, figs, raisins, pine kernels, wine, honey, and spices.

Originally, pies would have been formed with a simple flour and water dough as a pastry casing. These pie crusts were disposable vessels, made to encase and cook the contents and then to be discarded once the filling had been eaten. The pastry cast-offs would be given to servants or the poor.

Along with dried fruits, such as figs and dates, spices like ginger and saffron had to be imported into the country, so using any of these exotic ingredients would have shown a level of wealth and status. This combination of costly ingredients meant that mince pies were reserved for special occasions, feast days like

Easter or Christmas. These culinary creations were never intended for year-round consumption. This doesn't mean they were always small; medieval mince pies were often large enough to feed a family. Smaller versions of the mince pie were known as chewets, possibly named after the French chouette because the pinched pie tops resembled little cabbages.

Mince pies attract lots of myths, from the idea that they were once crib-shaped (they weren't), to the misconception that Oliver Cromwell banned them (he didn't). They had no specific religious connotations, but by the middle of the seventeenth century, they were undeniably associated with Christmas and feasting. By the end of the century, they were often made as individual pies, shaped geometrically and laid out like a very fashionable parterre garden.

Recipes from the Victorian era include shredded ox-tongue or lamb-tongue, but eventually, meat became a less prominent ingredient. The addition of more common ingredients like apples, raisins, and currants gave the pie a much sweeter profile. Suet has always remained the essential ingredient, giving the pie a light, pleasing texture. Modern vegetarian suet has become a common substitute, completely removing any trace of meat from our modern mince pie.

Today, around 800 million mince pies are eaten in the UK each Christmas.

Mince Pies

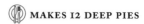

Preparation time 20 minutes plus 1 hour chilling time

Cooking time 35 minutes

The best thing about these mince pies is that they are made in good-sized tins – muffin tins are just right for the job. The result is that you get more filling than usual. The pastry is midway between the puff pastry and the more usual shortcrust; the glaze, containing just egg white and sugar, is unusual too. The original recipe doesn't specify how much sugar to use, but here there is lots, to give a really crisp, light crust to the top of the pies.

2 quantities flaky shortcrust pastry (see page 2)

plain flour, for dusting

600g lemon mincemeat

1 egg white

2 tbsp caster sugar

granulated sugar, for dredging

SPECIAL EQUIPMENT:

10cm and 5cm round pastry cutters

a deep 12-hole muffin tin

Make the flaky shortcrust pastry and chill it for 30 minutes. Just before the chilling time is over preheat the oven to 200°C/ gas mark 7.

Dust your work surface with flour and roll out the pastry to a thickness of 3mm. Stamp out 12 rounds 10cm in size and 12 rounds 5cm in size. You could even cut the smaller rounds into stars to top your pies.

Gently press each of the larger disks into one of the 12 holes of the muffin tin, making sure that the edge of the pastry sits slightly proud of the top edge. Divide the mincemeat evenly among the lined muffin-tin holes.

Moisten the edges of the small pastry discs and place each one on top of a pie. Crimp the edges of the pastry together to make a good seal to prevent the mincemeat boiling out. Whisk together the egg white and the caster sugar and brush this mixture over the tops of the pies. Dredge each pie with a little granulated sugar and pierce a hole in the centre of each lid with sharp knife or a skewer.

Bake for 10 minutes, or until well browned on top, then reduce the heat to 160°C/gas mark 4. Bake for a further 25 minutes, or until the pies are deep golden brown. Remove the tin from the oven and leave to cool for a few minutes on a wire rack. Then carefully lift the pies from the muffin tin while they are still warm and place on a cooling rack. They are delicious eaten warm with clotted cream. They can be stored in an airtight tin for up to 3 days.

Bakewell Pudding

 SERVES 6

Preparation time 20 minutes plus 30 minutes resting time

Cooking time 1 hour 25 minutes

This lovely pudding is a real treasure. Some classic recipes use puff pastry for Bakewell pudding, but a well-baked shortcrust tart case is a better match, giving a crisp contrast to the rich, silky filling. Use homemade raspberry jam if you have it, or choose a sharp conserve to contrast with the sweet filling.

½ quantity shortcrust pastry (see page 4)

FOR THE FILLING:

115g butter

160g caster sugar

30g ground almonds

5 egg yolks and 1 egg white

80g sharp, best-quality raspberry jam

SPECIAL EQUIPMENT:

a deep 22cm metal pie dish and some baking beans

First make the pastry and leave it to rest in the fridge for 20 minutes. Then, roll the pastry out on a floured surface to a 27cm round. Place it in the pie dish, leaving the extra pastry hanging over the edge. Line the pastry with a large piece of non-stick baking paper and then fill with baking beans. Leave to rest in a cool place for 10 minutes.

Preheat the oven to 200°C/gas mark 7.

Place the pastry case on a baking tray and bake for 35 minutes until firm and golden brown. Remove the beans and paper and return the case to the oven for 5 minutes to bake further and dry slightly. Remove from the oven and set aside. Reduce the oven to 160°C/gas mark 3.

Make the filling by melting the butter in a medium pan over a low heat. Remove from the heat, and add the sugar, ground almonds and eggs, beating well to combine.

Spread the jam into the pastry case and carefully pour over the filling. Bake for 15 minutes, then turn the oven to 140°C/gas mark 3 for a further 30 minutes until the filling is just firm to the touch. Trim the pastry hanging over the rim with a sharp knife and cool to room temperature before serving.

Chelsea Buns

MAKES 7

Preparation time 3 hours including rising time

Cooking time 20 minutes

---

1 quantity enriched dough
(see page 8)

100g softened unsalted butter,
plus a little extra for greasing

50g soft brown sugar

½ tsp freshly grated nutmeg

180g currants

4 tsp caster sugar, for dusting

SPECIAL EQUIPMENT:

a 25cm round spring-form
cake tin

Make the enriched bread dough and leave it to rest, covered, in a
warm place. After 15 minutes, dust your work surface with flour and
place the dough on top. Knead for about 10 minutes, or until the
dough feels smooth and satiny, then place it into a lightly oiled bowl,
cover with a clean, dry tea towel and leave to rise for 1–1½ hours, or
until almost doubled in size.

Meanwhile, make the filling by creaming together the butter, brown
sugar and grated nutmeg until pale and fluffy. Add the currants and
stir in well.

Grease the spring-form cake tin, line it with non-stick baking paper
and set it aside. When the dough is ready, place it on the lightly
floured work surface and press out to a flat sheet. Using a rolling pin,

roll to a rectangle about 30 x 35cm, allowing the dough to rest for a couple of minutes. If it shrinks back from the desired size, then re-roll until you have the dimensions specified.

With the longest edge facing you, spread the filling mixture evenly over the entire surface of the dough then roll the dough up into a tight cylinder. Trim the edges to neaten the roll then, at 5cm intervals, cut through the dough to make 7 equal rounds. Arrange 6 of the rounds, flat-side down and evenly spaced apart, around the inside edge of the prepared tin and place the remaining round in the centre. Cover with cling film and leave to rise in a warm place for 30 minutes, or until the rounds have increased in size by about half and are beginning to push up against each other. Towards the end of the rising time preheat the oven to 160°C/gas mark 4.

Remove the cling film from the buns, dust them with 2 teaspoons of caster sugar and bake for 20 minutes, or until the buns are golden brown. Once cooked, dust again with the remaining caster sugar, remove from the tin all in one piece, and cool before serving. The buns can be stored for 2–3 days in an airtight tin or frozen for up to 1 month.

Plum Frangipane Tart

 SERVES 8

⏱ Preparation time 15 minutes
plus 1 hour 30 minutes–2 hours 30 minutes chilling time

🍳 Cooking time 1 hour 20 minutes

This elegant tart presents a perfect balance of fruit to almond frangipane. Ground rice can be substituted for the almonds used here if you have a nut allergy – the resulting texture is pleasantly fine.

---

1 quantity sweet pastry
(see page 3)

150g softened unsalted butter

150g caster sugar

3 eggs

½ tsp almond extract

150g ground almonds

scant 2 tbsp plain flour, sifted,
plus extra for dusting

3 tbsp damson or plum jam

600g small purple plums,
stoned and quartered

2 tbsp flaked almonds

SPECIAL EQUIPMENT:

a 22cm loose-bottomed
tart tin

some baking beans

Make the sweet pastry, cover and chill for 1–2 hours. When it has finished chilling, roll the pastry out to a 30cm circle. Flour your fingers and transfer it to the tart tin, pressing it carefully into the bottom and allowing any extra pastry to hang over the edge. This helps to prevent shrinkage during cooking. Cover the tin loosely with cling film and chill for 20 minutes. Preheat the oven to 200°C/gas mark 7.

Line the chilled pastry case with non-stick baking paper and fill it with baking beans. Bake for 20 minutes, then turn the oven down to 160°C/gas mark 4 for a further 15–20 minutes, or until the pastry is cooked through.

Once the pastry case is cooked, remove the paper and beans from the tin carefully. If there are any cracks, roll some of the excess pastry trimmings between your fingers to make it pliable and use it to fill the gaps. Return the case to the oven and bake for a further 5 minutes, or until it is evenly brown, then remove it from the oven and set it on a wire rack to cool. Turn the oven up to 180°C/gas mark 6.

Cream the butter with the sugar until light and fluffy then mix in the eggs and almond extract. Fold in the ground almonds and sifted flour and set aside. Now spread the jam evenly over the bottom of the tart case. Pour in the almond mixture, spreading it to the edges to cover the jam, then arrange the quartered plums on top, pushing them lightly into the almond mixture. Sprinkle over the flaked almonds.

Bake for 35–40 minutes, or until the almond mixture is evenly browned and firm. Let it stand for a few minutes, then trim any excess pastry from the edges, remove the tart from the tin and leave to cool a little. Serve with clotted cream.

A History of
HOT CROSS BUNS

Our humble hot cross bun has become a fixture of our modern Easter celebrations. Spiced, fruit-filled bread, marked with a cross, has been part of our British culinary tradition for centuries. Its origins are a combination of religious observance and cultural custom

There are records of fruited buns being made at Easter in the Middle Ages, though the various modern-day claims to be the earliest don't tend to hold up to scrutiny. This includes the Alban Bun, supposedly given as alms at St Albans Abbey in the 1360s.

During the reign of Queen Elizabeth I, the practice of baking spiced buns became a tradition designated to specific dates. Elizabethan controls on the size, shape, and price of bread sold also limited the bakers, who were only permitted to make their buns on Good Friday, Christmas, or at funerals. A law prohibited the sale of fruit buns at any other time of year. This regulation increased the cultural and religious significance of the buns, associating them with particular occasions.

We know this reference to a 'cross bun' was written in a satirical almanac in 1671, "Good-Friday I foresee, will prove but a very bad day with such poor Christians that have neither a cross bun to put in their bellies, nor a Cross to put in their pockets."

By the 18th century, they were often sold hot, and vendors in the streets would call out, "One a penny, two a penny. Hot cross buns," to attract customers. The nursery rhyme gained popularity, reflecting how the buns had become a widespread cultural tradition.

In the last century, the cross on the bun has been made of plain flour paste instead of being cut into the dough, keeping the religious connection to this Easter time treat. Eating a hot cross bun on Good Friday is still a significant act for those of the Christian faith; the bread represents the wafer used in holy Communion, and the cross is seen as a direct reference to the crucifixion.

Today, hot cross buns can be enjoyed all year round, although they are especially popular during the Easter period. During this time of year, in supermarkets across the UK, many new and unusual flavour combinations appear, including savoury cheese versions, salted caramel and chocolate, strawberries and cream, and even a banoffee flavour.

Hot Cross Buns

Preparation time 3 hours including rising and resting time

Cooking time 15–20 minutes

---

1 quantity enriched dough (see page 8) but made with 7g dried yeast and an extra 25g butter

30g raisins

50g chopped mixed peel

25g sultanas

1 tsp mixed spice

1 tsp ground cinnamon

flour, for dusting

FOR THE CROSS PASTE:

100g plain flour

20g caster sugar

for the glaze

50g apricot jam

1 tbsp caster sugar

SPECIAL EQUIPMENT:

a piping bag fitted with a small round nozzle

Make the dough as directed, with a little extra yeast, then add an additional 25g melted butter at the end.

After 15 minutes resting, uncover the dough and add the raisins, chopped mixed peel, sultanas, mixed spice and ground cinnamon. Blend them in by breaking up the dough and kneading in the ingredients. When fully combined, turn the dough out onto a lightly floured work surface and knead for 10 minutes, or until it feels soft and smooth and the added ingredients are evenly distributed. The dough should feel slightly tacky but not sticky. Add a little flour as you knead if it is too sticky. Shape the dough into a round and place it in a lightly oiled bowl. Cover with a clean, dry tea towel and leave to rise in a warm place for 1–1½ hours, or until almost doubled in size.

Line a baking tray with non-stick baking paper. Flour your work surface and place the dough onto it. Divide the dough evenly into 8 pieces, shape each one into a round ball and arrange them on the baking tray, spaced about 2cm apart and covered loosely with cling film. Leave in a warm place for 30 minutes, or until almost doubled in size.

Meanwhile, preheat the oven to 180°C/gas mark 6 and make the cross paste. Sift the flour and sugar into a bowl, add 75ml water and mix to a thick, smooth paste. Place this into a piping bag fitted with a small round nozzle and pipe a cross onto each bun. Bake for 15–20 minutes, or until the buns are golden brown. While the buns are baking make the glaze. Place a small pan over a medium heat. Add the apricot jam, caster sugar and 50ml water. Heat until simmering, then cook until the sugar and jam have dissolved and the mixture has reduced by one-third.

Using a pastry brush, paint the glaze onto the buns as they come out of the oven. Serve immediately, split open and spread with salted butter, or store in an airtight tin for up to 3 days. The buns can also be frozen for up to 1 month.

Cakes

Victoria Sponge

Preparation time 30 minutes

Cooking time 25 minutes

Here's a yummy recipe for Victoria Sponge with jam and cream.

FOR THE SPONGES:

240g unsalted butter softened, plus extra for greasing

240g caster sugar, plus extra to dust the cake with

4 eggs, lightly beaten

2 tsp vanilla extract

240g self raising flour, sifted

3–4 tbsp milk

FOR THE FILLING:

200ml double cream

2 tbsp icing sugar, plus extra for dusting

5 tbsp raspberry jam

SPECIAL EQUIPMENT:

2 x 20cm sandwich tins

Preheat the oven to 180°C/gas mark 6

Grease and line the bases of 2 x 20cm sandwich tins.

Cream butter and sugar together until pale and fluffy, add the beaten egg a little at a time, beating it into the mixture until all incorporated.

Stir in the vanilla extract then fold in the flour gently. Divide the mix between the two tins and level off using a spatula or palette knife.

Bake the cakes in the oven for around 25 minutes, until a skewer inserted in the centre comes out clean.

Remove cakes from oven and leave to rest in the tins for five minutes.

Remove sponges from the tins, remove lining paper and place sponges on a wire rack to cool.

Whisk the double cream with the icing sugar until soft peaks form, sandwich the jam and cream between the two cooled sponges, sprinkle with caster sugar and top with fresh raspberries, if desired, and enjoy.

Citrus Pound Cake

 SERVES 6–8

Preparation time 15 minutes

Cooking time 1 hour

This pound cake uses a little almond and citrus to scent the crumb. It is a lovely mixture and quite fine on its own, without icing or fillings. The simple combination is perfect with a cup of Earl Grey tea.

230g softened unsalted butter, plus extra for greasing

230g caster sugar

4 medium eggs at room temperature

½ tsp almond extract

280g self-raising flour, sifted, plus extra for dusting the tin

70g candied peel, cut into small chunks

25g ground almonds

SPECIAL EQUIPMENT:

a deep cake tin, 20cm round or 17cm square

Preheat the oven to 160°C/gas mark 4. Grease the tin with a little soft butter, then line the base with non-stick baking paper.

In a large bowl, beat the butter until light and soft. Add the caster sugar and cream together until the mixture is light and fluffy and the sugar is well incorporated.

Beat the eggs lightly with the almond extract to break them up.

Then add this mixture, 2 tablespoons at a time, to the butter and sugar mixture, beating well after each addition. When two-thirds of the egg mixture has been incorporated, fold in 1 tablespoon of sifted flour using a large metal spoon. Fold in the remaining egg mixture and then sift in the remaining flour. Add the cut peel and almonds and fold everything together until all the ingredients are well distributed, but working gently to retain the lightness of the batter.

Pour the batter into the prepared tin and make a small depression in the centre. Place in the centre of the oven for 40 minutes, then reduce the heat to 150°C/gas mark 3 and bake for a further 20–25 minutes, or until the cake is firm to a light touch and a skewer inserted into the middle of the cake comes out clean. Or, insert a temperature probe into the centre of the cake. If it registers 95°C the cake is done.

Remove from the oven and cool the cake for 10 minutes in the tin before transferring to a wire cooling rack. When it is completely cool, store it in an airtight container. The lovely flavour of this cake develops further if it is left for 2–3 days before serving.

DOWN HOUSE

Down House was the Darwin family home, where Charles Darwin lived for forty years with his wife Emma and their growing family. When the couple bought the property in 1842, they were unimpressed with the house. The grounds were of significant interest to Charles, as the landscape contained both London clay and the chalk of north Kent. After landscaping, the garden became a productive area for his scientific research; a place to breed fancy pigeons and study the flight of bumble bees. In 1859, he published 'On the Origin of Species by Means of Natural Selection', which is still considered one of the most profound contributions to science.

Today, the grounds have been restored to their former glory by the English Heritage. You can smell the scent of azaleas, Emma Darwin's favourite flower, and appreciate her informal planting style in the garden. This lack of Victorian stuffiness and formality extended to their family life. The Darwins encouraged their children to have fun and explore, from sliding down the stairs indoors to enjoying all the natural wonders outside. In some of their memoirs, the Darwin children remembered a childhood full of mischief, with trees to climb and dozens of pets to play with.

The landscape became a living laboratory for Darwin and the base for all of his research in later life. A glass house was constructed and heated by coal to a temperature of eighteen degrees centigrade, to grow tropical orchids and carnivorous plants so that Darwin could study the evolutionary adaptation of plants.

Charles Darwin also created a kitchen garden that would provide for his growing family and a household of staff. This cultivated area was full of vegetables and fruit trees, but also a mix of culinary and medicinal herbs. It provided seasonal produce for the kitchens where Emma Darwin took an active role in the daily preparation of food. Months after her marriage in 1839, Emma began to write down recipes for home cooking. Over the years, friends and relatives added dishes, Charles himself wrote instructions for boiling rice, and their daughter Annie added two recipes. The book contains shopping lists, hints and tips from other women and chefs, and a multitude of dessert recipes. With a large family to feed and some homegrown Kentish apples, Mrs Darwin's baked apple pudding must have been a treat for all the family.

Apple cake

 SERVES 8

Preparation time 20 minutes

Cooking time 1 hour

---

4 eating apples – peeled &
cored and cut into rough
2.5cm chunks

1 tsp of ground cinnamon

2 tbsp of granulated sugar

230g plain flour

½ tbsp baking powder

½ tsp of salt

125ml sunflower oil

200g granulated sugar

1 tsp of vanilla extract

3 eggs

Preheat the oven to 160°C/gas mark 4. Line a 22cm loose bottom tin.

Mix the apples, cinnamon and sugar in a small bowl. Leave while you prepare the cake mixture.

In a large bowl mix the flour, baking powder and salt.

In another bowl whisk the oil, sugar, vanilla extract and the eggs until they are thoroughly mixed. Add the flour mixture to the oil mixture and mix thoroughly.

Place half the cake batter into the cooking tin. Place half the apple mix and juices on top of the cake batter. Cover with the rest of the cake batter. Place the rest of the apple mixture evenly over the surface of the cake.

Bake for 55–60 minutes – cover with tin foil and bake for another 10 minutes if not done.

Leave to cool in the tin before turning it out.

TWELFTH NIGHT CAKE

Christmas can trace some of its origins to the Roman festival of Saturnalia, when a tribute to Saturn, the Roman God of agriculture, took place around the winter solstice. It may also have pagan roots in various festivals celebrating the year's turning point with fires, feasting and often riotous partying. Christians eventually adopted the festivities, which evolved into Christmas, a celebration of the birth of Christ. The feasting went on for twelve nights until Epiphany on the night before the 6th of January. 'Twelfth Night', as it was known, was a particular focus for games involving social upheaval – boy bishops, girl abbesses, and master and servant swapping roles.

By the reign of Elizabeth I, it also involved a celebratory cake, which was typically a rich, yeasty fruit bread flavoured with spices, with a token or bean hidden inside. The person who found the bean became the Lord of Misrule or King of the Bean, and they'd have to organise the evening's revelry.

After the Reformation, the religious festival of

Epiphany almost vanished, but the cake prevailed. The tokens evolved to encompass a much bigger range of symbols, and, eventually, some printers started producing special Twelfth Night character cards, complete with riddles or jokes.

People began to use eggs to raise the cake, and as sugar and fruit came down in price, the cake became less of a fruited bread and more like the rich fruit cake we know today. By the end of the Georgian period, the cake was often decorated with almond paste and elaborate moulded sugar figures.

By the Victorian era, Epiphany celebrations included masquerades, gambling, and a lot of alcohol. Middle-class writers trying to remake Christmas as a family festival disapproved of such raucous revelry, and the Twelfth Night Cake gradually evolved into the Christmas Cake. Nevertheless, Queen Victoria shared a Twelfth Cake with local children until the very end of her life.

In parts of Spain, France, and the Caribbean, variations of the cake are still enjoyed as a part of the festivities for Epiphany, sometimes known as the 'Feast of the Three Kings'. Some Twelfth Night Cakes are more like filled pastries, while others might be ring-shaped and topped with crystallised fruits. They come complete with a small ceramic figure as the token, and foil crowns for the finder to wear.

Twelfth Night Cake

 SERVES 10

Preparation time 20 minutes

Cooking time 2½ hours

225g butter

225g dark muscovado sugar

1 tbsp black treacle

225g plain flour

1 tsp mixed spice

4 large eggs

225g raisins

225g currants

225g sultanas

50g chopped mixed peel

50g glacé cherries, halved

50g ground almonds

1 tbsp brandy

Preheat the oven to 160°C/gas mark 3.

Cream the butter and sugar together until light and fluffy and then beat in the treacle.

Sift the flour, spice and a pinch of salt into the bowl. Lightly whisk the eggs with a fork and then beat them gently into the butter and sugar mixture, together with the flour. When thoroughly mixed, stir in the fruits, nuts and brandy and then pile into a greased and lined 18cm round cake tin.

Place in the centre of the oven. Bake for approximately 1½ hours, then reduce the temperature to 120°C/gas mark ½ and bake for a further 1 hour or until the cake is well risen, golden brown and firm to the touch. A skewer inserted into the centre should come out cleanly.

Leave the cake to cool in the tin, covered with a clean cloth. Turn out when completely cold.

You can decorate yours with a crown to symbolise the King of the Bean, but if you're feeling creative you could use almond paste/marzipan and sugar icing like a traditional Christmas cake.

Queen's Pudding

 SERVES 4–6

🕐 *Preparation time 50 minutes* 🍳 *Cooking time 45–55 minutes*

Of all the flavoured milk and breadcrumb puddings that crop up in the British repertoire, this one is the best. It is very similar to Manchester pudding but requires no pastry, so is quicker to make for the time-pressured cook. The lemon-scented base contrasts perfectly with the raspberry jam and light meringue topping.

650ml milk

25g unsalted butter, plus extra for greasing

25g caster sugar

seeds scraped from one vanilla pod

110g stale white bread or cake crumbs

finely grated zest of 1½ lemons

pinch freshly grated nutmeg

4 egg yolks

200g sharp raspberry jam

FOR THE MERINGUE TOPPING:

6 egg whites

300g caster sugar

SPECIAL EQUIPMENT:

a deep, 22cm pie dish

a roasting tin

Place the milk, butter, sugar and vanilla seeds in a saucepan over a medium heat and bring almost to simmering. Remove from the heat and leave for the flavour to infuse for 30 minutes.

Preheat the oven to 160°C/gas mark 4. Butter the pie dish.

Place the bread or cake crumbs, lemon zest and nutmeg into a large bowl and combine. Pour in the infused milk and mix together.

Fill the kettle and bring it to the boil.

Lightly beat the egg yolks and add them a little at a time to the bread mixture until fully incorporated. Then pour the mixture into a buttered baking dish and place in a roasting tin.

Pour boiling water into the roasting tin to a depth of 2cm and bake for 35–45 minutes, or until set. Remove from oven and spread the raspberry jam over the top.

Turn the oven up to 200°C/gas mark 7.

Make the meringue topping by placing the egg whites into the bowl of a mixer and beating them quickly for 2 minutes. Add the sugar and beat to make a stiff meringue. Pile this over the layer of jam, spreading the meringue carefully right to the edges of the dish. Bake for 10 minutes, or until the pudding turns golden brown on top.

Allow the pudding to cool a little before serving.

Caraway Seed Cake

 SERVES 6–8

Preparation time 20 minutes

Cooking time 1 hour–1 hour 20 minutes

This recipe adds a little brandy to the seed cake – a lovely addition, and quite the height of sophistication. The original historical recipe has been altered here only in that the proportion of flour has been reduced to show just how little you can get away with – the resulting crumb is moist and lighter than the citrus pound cake on page 36.

230g softened unsalted butter, plus extra for greasing

200g caster sugar

3 medium eggs at room temperature

75ml brandy

200g self-raising flour, sifted

1 tsp caraway seeds

pinch ground mace

few gratings of nutmeg

SPECIAL EQUIPMENT:
a 1kg loaf tin

Preheat the oven to 160°C/gas mark 4. Grease the loaf tin with a little soft butter and line it with non-stick baking paper, leaving an overhang of 2cm on the long sides to help you lift the cake out of the tin when it is baked.

In a large bowl, beat the butter until it is very soft. Add the sugar and cream together until light and fluffy.

Lightly beat the eggs and brandy together then add this mixture, 2 tablespoons at a time, to the butter mixture, beating well after each addition. When two-thirds of the egg mixture has been incorporated, fold in 1 tablespoon of sifted flour using a large metal spoon. Then fold the remaining egg mixture into the batter.

Mix the caraway seeds and the spices with the remaining flour and sift over the batter. Fold it in carefully until there are no lumps. Pour the batter into the prepared loaf tin.

Place in the centre of the oven for 40–50 minutes, then reduce the heat to 150°C/gas mark 3, and bake for a further 25–30 minutes, or until the loaf is a deep golden brown. The loaf is ready when a thin skewer pushed into the centre comes out clean, or a temperature probe registers 95°C. If it is not cooked but is browning too much, turn the temperature down to 130°C/gas mark 2 and cover the top of the loaf with a piece of foil. Test again after 10 minutes.

When it is done remove from the oven and cool in the tin for 10 minutes. Transfer the cake to a wire rack to cool completely before storing in an airtight container.

Battenburg

 SERVES 8

🕐 *Preparation time 60 minutes*

🍳 *Cooking time 30 minutes*

FOR ALMOND SPONGE:

175g very soft butter

175g golden caster sugar

140g self-raising flour

50g ground almonds

½ tsp baking powder

3 medium eggs

½ tsp vanilla extract

¼ tsp almond extract

FOR PINK SPONGE:

1 x ingredients for almond sponge

½ tsp pink food colouring

TO ASSEMBLE:

200g apricot jam

2 x blocks white marzipan

a little icing sugar, for dusting

SPECIAL EQUIPMENT:

a 20cm square tin

Preheat oven to 180°C/gas mark 6 and line the base and sides of a 20cm square tin with baking parchment (the easiest way is to cross 2 x 20cm-long strips over the base). To make the almond sponge, put the butter, sugar, flour, ground almonds, baking powder, eggs, vanilla and almond extract in a large bowl. Beat with an electric whisk until the mix comes together smoothly. Scrape into the tin, spreading to the corners, and bake for 25–30 minutes – when you poke in a skewer, it should come out clean. Cool in the tin for 10 minutes, then transfer to a wire rack to finish cooling while you make the second sponge.

For the pink sponge, line the tin as above. Mix all the ingredients together as above, but don't add the almond extract. Fold in some pink food colouring. Then scrape it all into the tin and bake as before. Cool.

To assemble, heat the jam in a small pan until runny, then sieve. Barely trim two opposite edges from the almond sponge, then well trim a third edge. Roughly measure the height of the sponge, then, cutting from the well-trimmed edge, use a ruler to help you cut 4 slices each the same width as the sponge height. Discard or nibble leftover sponge. Repeat with the pink cake.

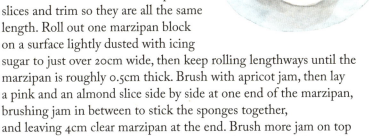

Take 2 x almond slices and 2 x pink slices and trim so they are all the same length. Roll out one marzipan block on a surface lightly dusted with icing sugar to just over 20cm wide, then keep rolling lengthways until the marzipan is roughly 0.5cm thick. Brush with apricot jam, then lay a pink and an almond slice side by side at one end of the marzipan, brushing jam in between to stick the sponges together, and leaving 4cm clear marzipan at the end. Brush more jam on top of the sponges, then sandwich remaining 2 slices on top, alternating colours to give a checkerboard effect. Trim the marzipan to the length of the cakes.

Carefully lift up the marzipan and smooth over the cake with your hands, but leave a small marzipan fold along the bottom edge before you stick it to the first side. Trim opposite side to match size of fold, then crimp edges using fingers and thumb (or, more simply, press with prongs of a fork).

Lemon Sponge

⏱ Preparation time 20 minutes

🍳 Cooking time 40 minutes

This versatile cake is especially nice served sliced with English Heritage All Butter Lemon Curd and whipped cream. However, it can also be used, sliced and layered, in a trifle (see page 114 and note below) and the crumbs can be used in the queen's pudding on page 46.

25g unsalted butter, melted, plus a little extra for greasing

4 medium eggs

115g caster sugar

1 tbsp orange flower water

finely grated zest of ½ lemon

115g plain flour, sifted

SPECIAL EQUIPMENT:

a deep 20cm round cake tin

Preheat the oven to 180°C/gas mark 6. Grease the cake tin with a little soft butter, then line the base with non-stick baking paper.

Using an electric mixer, whisk the eggs for a minute then add the sugar and orange flower water. Beat at high speed for 10–15 minutes until the mixture is light and mousse-like.

Working quickly but gently, fold in the lemon zest and flour, and then the melted butter. Make sure all the ingredients are well incorporated and there are no lumps.

Pour the batter into the prepared tin and place in the centre of the oven. After 25 minutes turn the oven down to 160°C/gas mark 4 for a further 15 minutes. The cake is cooked when it is evenly browned all over or firm to a light touch and a skewer inserted into the middle of the cake comes out clean. Or, insert a temperature probe into the centre of the cake. If it registers 95°C the cake is done.

Note: If you are planning to bake this cake for use in the trifle recipe, use the method above but with the quantities given below, and bake in a 23cm square cake tin. The cake will take 25 minutes to bake at 180°C/gas mark 6.

20g unsalted butter, melted, plus a little extra for greasing

3 medium eggs

85g caster sugar

½–1 tbsp orange flower water

zest of ⅓ lemon

85g plain flour

Swiss Roll

 SERVES 8

Preparation time 10 minutes

Cooking time 10 minutes

The Swiss Roll, with its delicate sponge cake and swirl of sweet filling, has been a beloved dessert for generations. Despite its name, the Swiss Roll likely has roots in Austria, where it is known as the 'Jelly Roll' and has been a part of European baking for centuries. The Swiss name came into play in the 19th century, perhaps due to the popularity of Swiss pâtissiers at the time.

4 eggs

100g caster sugar

100g self-raising flour

Icing sugar for sprinkling

Jam for filling (you could use English Heritage Strawberry and Champagne Preserve)

SPECIAL EQUIPMENT:

a swiss roll tin (33x 23cm)

Preheat the oven to 220°C/gas mark 9 and grease a swiss roll tin (33x 23cm) and line with baking paper.

Beat the eggs and sugar together until light and frothy and then sift in the flour, carefully folding it into the mixture.

Pour the mixture into the tin and bake for around 10 minutes, until it's lightly browned and coming away from the tin at the edges.

Place some baking paper on a work surface and sprinkle with icing sugar, before upending the sponge from the tin and peeling off the baking paper. Neaten the edges and leave to cool.

Spread with jam and score the sponge lightly 2.5cm from one end. Roll carefully. Neaten up the ends with a knife.

Carrot Cake

SERVES 8

⏱ Preparation time 30 minutes

🍳 Cooking time 1 hour 15 minutes

A true classic. Historically, carrots were used as an alternative to expensive imported dried fruits. Carrot has been used in dishes as an alternative to refined sugar as far back as the middle ages.

FOR THE CAKE:

225ml sunflower oil, plus extra to grease

225g light muscovado sugar

4 medium eggs

225g self-raising flour

1 tsp bicarbonate of soda

1½ tsp each mixed spice, ground cinnamon and ground ginger

150g sultanas

200g carrots, coarsely grated

50–75g walnuts or pecans, roughly chopped

FOR THE ICING:

175g unsalted butter, very soft

1 tsp vanilla extract

275g full-fat cream cheese, at room temperature

200g icing sugar

SPECIAL EQUIPMENT:

a 20cm cake tin

Preheat the oven to 140°C / gas mark 3. Grease a 20cm cake tin and line both the base and sides with parchment paper. In a large bowl, whisk together the oil, sugar and eggs until the mixture is smooth.

Add the flour, bicarbonate of soda, and spices, then mix until well combined. Stir in the sultanas, grated carrots and chopped nuts. Pour the batter into the prepared tin, level the surface, and bake for 1 hour 5 minutes to 1 hour 15 minutes, or until a skewer inserted into the centre comes out clean. Allow the cake to cool in the tin for 5 minutes before turning it out onto a wire rack to cool completely.

For the icing, beat the butter and vanilla in a large bowl until smooth. Add the cream cheese (make sure it's at room temperature) and mix until fully incorporated. Sift in the icing sugar and beat – start slowly to avoid a cloud of sugar – until the icing is smooth and fluffy.

Once the cake is completely cool, slice it horizontally through the middle. Use half of the icing to sandwich the two layers together and place the cake on a serving plate or stand. Spread the remaining icing over the top. Slice to serve.

Coffee and Walnut Cake

SERVES 8

⏲ *Preparation time 20 minutes*

🍳 *Cooking time 25 minutes*

---

2 tbsp instant coffee

120g walnut halves

230g butter, at room temperature

230g soft, light-brown sugar

4 eggs, beaten together

230g plain flour

3 tsp baking powder

¼ tsp salt

Milk, optional

FOR THE ICING:

2 tbsp instant coffee

170g butter, at room temperature

430g icing sugar

¼ tsp salt

4 tbsp milk

SPECIAL EQUIPMENT:

2 x 20cm sandwich tins

Preheat the oven to 180°C / gas mark 6 and grease and line the bases of 2 x 20cm sandwich tins.

Mix the coffee with 1 tablespoon of boiling water, and then leave to cool. Meanwhile, toast the walnut halves in a dry pan or oven until toasted, then set half of them aside and chop up the remainder.

Cream the butter and sugar until light and fluffy. With the mixer still running, pour in the eggs slowly, scraping down the sides of the mixer as necessary. Once mixed, sift in the flour, baking powder and salt, and gently fold in. Then stir in your coffee and chopped walnuts.

The batter should be a dropping consistency; if it is too thick, add a splash of milk. Divide the mixture between the 2 tins and bake for about 25 minutes until well risen. Allow to cool for 10 minutes in the tins, then put on a wire rack to cool completely. Meanwhile, mix the 2 tablespoons of coffee for the icing with 1 tablespoon of boiling water and allow to cool.

To make the icing, beat the butter until soft, then sift in the sugar and salt and add the cooled coffee and cream. Stir together until evenly combined. Top one cake with a little less than half the icing, spreading it more thickly in a ring around the edge, and then place the other cake on top. Spoon the remaining icing on the top and arrange the walnut halves on top.

Butterfly Cakes

 MAKES 12

Preparation time 15 minutes

Cooking time 20 minutes

Butterfly cakes are a delightful twist on classic cupcakes, known for their signature wings made from the tops of the sponge. Light, airy, and often filled with buttercream and jam, they've been a staple at children's parties and afternoon teas for generations.

100g self raising flour

pinch salt

100g butter

100g caster

2 eggs

FOR THE CREAM:

150ml double cream

1 tsp caster sugar

¼ tsp vanilla extract

icing sugar, for dusting

SPECIAL EQUIPMENT:

a piping bag with a large star nozzle

Grease 12 hole muffin/bun tin, or line with cupcake cases. Preheat the oven to 180°C/gas mark 6. Mix the flour and salt in a bowl.

In a mixing bowl, cream the butter with the sugar until light and fluffy. Beat in the eggs, then lightly stir in the flour and salt.

Divide the mixture evenly between the prepared bun tins and bake for 15–20 minutes until golden. Cool on a wire rack.

In a bowl, whip the cream with the caster sugar and vanilla extract until stiff. Transfer to a piping bag with a large star nozzle.

When the cakes are cool, cut a round off the top of each. Cut each round in half to create two 'butterfly wings'.

Pipe a star of cream on each cake, then add the 'wings', placing them cut side down and slightly apart. Dust with icing sugar.

Pancakes

 MAKES 12–15

🕐 *Preparation time 10 minutes plus 10 minutes resting time*

🍳 *Cooking time 30–45 minutes*

This basic pancake recipe was accompanied by the note that 'pancakes are almost never good unless eaten almost immediately after they come from the frying pan' – advice worth heeding. They were served with 'sifted sugar and a cut lemon', much as we do in Britain today.

225g plain flour
600ml milk
3 medium eggs
small pinch salt
large pinch caster sugar
25g butter, melted
50g butter, to cook

TO SERVE:
caster sugar or honey
lemon wedges

SPECIAL EQUIPMENT:
a 17–20cm frying pan
or crêpe pan

Mix the flour, milk and eggs together with the salt and sugar in a bowl. Whisk until the batter is free of lumps, then leave to stand in a cool place for at least 10 minutes, or until required.

Strain the batter through a fine sieve into a jug and stir in the melted butter.

Line the frying pan with ½ teaspoon of butter and set it over a medium to high heat. When it is hot, pour in a little batter, swirling the pan to encourage the batter to cover the entire base. Cook the pancake for 1–2 minutes on each side, or until it is golden brown and firm. Remove to a plate. If you are not serving the pancakes immediately, layer them with non-stick baking paper and keep them warm on a plate in a low oven. Continue making pancakes until all of the batter has been used up.

To reheat, simply drop each pancake back into a hot pan and cook for 30 seconds on each side.

Serve with a sprinkling of sugar or honey and a squeeze of lemon.

SOUL CAKES

Soul cakes were traditionally given to children or poor people, known as 'soulers', who would go from door to door, singing songs or reciting prayers in exchange for these tasty treats. 'Souling' is an old English tradition that dates back five hundred years, with written references from 1511. The custom takes place around the collective days of Allhallowtide. This period stretched from October 31st, All Hallows' Eve (now known as Halloween), All Saints' Day on November 1st, and All Souls' Day on November 2nd, one of the holiest days in the Christian calendar. Sometimes known as Soul-mass Cakes, these sweet treats were thought to represent the souls of the departed; the act of giving one could help a lost soul move from purgatory into heaven and was considered a great act of charity.

Soul cakes varied in appearance and texture, and before the 19th century, it's very unclear what form they took at all. Folklorists collecting local customs recorded some soul cakes, even as the custom died out, reporting that they might be round or triangular, containing fruit, oats, or seeds added to represent the end of the harvest. They were mainly associated with the north of England.

The ritual of souling may have originated from Pagan autumn rituals or early Christian practices in England. In some areas, souling might have been linked to 'mumming' traditions, where people dress in costumes representing spirits of the dead and perform songs or plays in exchange for food and gifts. These practices spread across Scotland, Ireland, and Wales over the years, but it was most closely associated with England, especially the Black Country. While souling customs are not widely practiced in England today, in some local areas, the tradition of giving out soul cakes may still be part of modern Halloween celebrations.

In other parts of the world, variations of the souling practice have continued over the centuries. Pangangaluwa is a ritual in the Philippines, where children sing or pray for alms or cakes. In Portugal, soul cakes are known as Pao-por-Deus, which translates as 'bread for God'. Of course, the souling ritual is strikingly similar to the modern 'trick or treat' custom that occurs during Halloween in the United States, when sweets are given to children in costume on the doorstep.

Soul Cakes

 MAKES 30

🕐 *Preparation time 15 minutes*

🍲 *Cooking time 25 minutes*

300g plain flour, plus extra for dusting

2 tsp ground mixed spice

A pinch of nutmeg

150g butter, diced

150g caster sugar

75g currants

2 egg yolks (or 1 whole egg, beaten)

2 tbsp milk

1 tbsp oats

½ tbsp cider vinegar

SPECIAL EQUIPMENT:

a 6cm to 7cm round cutter

Preheat the oven to 180°C/gas mark 6. Sift the flour, spices and a pinch of salt into a mixing bowl, then add the butter and rub in with your fingers. Stir in the oats, currants and sugar.

Whisk the egg, milk and cider vinegar together until just combined, then stir into the dry ingredients. Bring together into a soft dough, and add more milk if the dough is too dry.

On a floured surface, roll out to about 5mm thick. Stamp out the soul cakes with a 6cm to 7cm round cutter, and score a cross lightly on the top. Transfer to two greased baking trays.

Bake for 15–25 minutes until pale golden brown. Cool on a wire rack.

Rock Cakes

 MAKES 12

Preparation time 10 minutes

Cooking time 20 minutes

Rock cakes may not win any beauty contests, but what they lack in looks, they more than make up for in charm and history. These crumbly, fruit-studded delights date back to the 19th century and earned their place as a staple in British baking. Originally created as a frugal treat, rock cakes became especially popular during World War II, when rationing called for simple ingredients and minimal sugar.

250g self-raising flour

65g raw sugar

¼ tsp cinnamon

90g butter

75g sultanas

75g mixed peel (or substitute with more sultanas)

1 egg

80ml milk

extra sugar, for sprinkling

Preheat the oven to about 180°C/gas mark 6. Grease a baking tray or cookie sheet with butter.

Sift flour, sugar and cinnamon together in a bowl. Using your fingertips, rub in the butter until the mixture resembles fine breadcrumbs.

Add the sultanas and mixed peel and mix well, breaking up clumps.

Beat the egg and add. Add sufficient milk to make a moist but stiff consistency. Depending on the flour you may need a little less or a little more milk.

Spoon mixture into rough walnut-sized lumps onto the greased tray. Leave space for slight spreading. Sprinkle with sugar.

Bake for 15–20 minutes or until cooked through.

Loosen on trays while hot and allow to cool or eat warm with or without butter.

Welsh Cakes

 **MAKES 15 CAKES**

🕐 *Preparation time 10 minutes*

🍳 *Cooking time 30–35 minutes*

Many classic recipes use dripping or lard for small cakes. The lard gives a 'short' dough that is best eaten warm with salted butter. Bilberry jam, common still in upland areas, makes the perfect accompaniment. Visit any Welsh market town and you will be able to buy these wonderful little cakes. They are often served with jam made from bilberries, which can be found growing on the upland heaths of Wales in the autumn.

150g self-raising flour, plus extra for dusting

pinch salt

50g caster sugar

½ tsp mixed spice

50g lard

30g currants

30g sultanas

1 egg

2 tbsp milk

SPECIAL EQUIPMENT:

a non-stick griddle or frying pan

a 6.5cm round pastry cutter

Place flour, salt, sugar, mixed spice and lard in a food processor. Blend for 2 minutes or until evenly mixed.

Transfer to a bowl and stir in the currants and sultanas. In another bowl, beat the egg and milk together and pour them into the flour mixture. Using a large fork, quickly but gently fold everything together.

Scatter some flour on your work surface and dust your fingers with flour. Place the mixture onto the floured surface and bring it together into a ball using your hands. Scatter some flour on your rolling pin and roll the dough out to a thickness of 4mm. Stamp 15 rounds out of the dough using the cutter.

Preheat the griddle or frying pan on a medium–low heat then add the cakes a few at a time. Cook the cakes for 4–5 minutes, or until the undersides are golden brown. Turn the cakes over using a spatula and cook the other side. Transfer the finished cakes to a wire rack to cool while you cook the rest.

Serve with unsalted butter and either jam or honey. These cakes can be stored in an airtight tin for up to 4 days or frozen for up to 1 month.

Anglo-Saxon Cakes

 MAKES 12

🕐 *Preparation time 10 minutes*

🍳 *Cooking time 12 minutes*

A lot of the food eaten by Anglo-Saxons will still be familiar to us today. As well as hunting and fishing, they kept livestock and farmed the land. The main crops they grew were barley, rye and wheat. They also ate dairy products such as milk, cheese and eggs. Sugar hadn't been discovered yet, so to sweeten their puddings, the Anglo-Saxons used dried fruits and honey. Small cakes, such as the ones here, would have been cooked in a heavy iron saucepan with a lid over a fire.

250g Scottish porridge oats

125g unsalted butter, plus extra for greasing

50g chopped dried apricots or dried apples

4 large tbsp runny honey

1 level tsp of ground cinnamon

Preheat the oven to 180°C/gas mark 6. Melt the butter in a large saucepan and remove from the heat. Add the honey, oats, cinnamon and dried fruit to the butter and stir until everything is well mixed.

Grease a baking tray, spoon 12 dollops of the mixture on it and then flatten them slightly. Bake in the oven for 10–12 minutes.

Place the cakes onto a wire rack and leave to cool before eating.

Dark Chocolate Cake

 SERVES 6–8

🕐 *Preparation time 15 minutes*

🍳 *Cooking time 20 minutes*

This is a variation on a chocolate soufflé recipe, which appears in its original form on page 122. This cake uses whole rather than separated eggs, and includes butter. Those two elements combine to give a fudgy texture that is fantastic when served just warm, with whipped cream on the side.

150g slightly salted butter, plus extra for greasing

40g cocoa powder, plus extra for dusting

200g plain dark chocolate (65–70% cocoa solids)

5 medium eggs, at room temperature

1 egg yolk, at room temperature

70g soft brown sugar

150g caster sugar

3 tbsp brandy

90g plain flour

SPECIAL EQUIPMENT:

a deep 23cm round spring-form cake tin

a large heatproof bowl

Preheat the oven to 160°C/gas mark 4. Grease the cake tin with a little soft butter, then pour some cocoa powder into the tin, rolling it around to coat the inside and tipping out any excess. Then line the base with non-stick baking paper.

Place the butter and chocolate in a large heatproof bowl and set it over a pan of barely simmering water on a low heat. Do not allow the bottom of the bowl to touch the water. Leave the chocolate to melt without stirring.

Place the eggs, egg yolk and sugars in the bowl of an electric mixer. Beat at high speed for 10–15 minutes, or until light and creamy, then add the brandy and beat until combined.

Sieve the cocoa and flour together. Working quickly but gently, fold the cocoa mixture into the egg mixture using a large metal spoon, ensuring that there are no lumps or bits of dry flour.

Pour the batter into the prepared tin and bake for 20 minutes. Once cooked, allow the cake to cool in the tin, then carefully remove the sides of the tin and slice with a sharp knife dipped in hot water.

The cake will remain deliciously moist and fudgy in the middle. Serve it at room temperature with some whipped cream and fresh raspberries on the side.

Teatime Treats

A History Of
AFTERNOON TEA

Afternoon tea is a refined British ritual that has evolved over the years. Modern offerings include a range of delicate sandwiches, buttery scones with fresh clotted cream, and elegant cakes, served on fine china.

Its origins lie in the late 18th century, and relate to the rituals of wealthy ladies, who would visit each other to take tea in the afternoon. Tea was invariably accompanied by light cakes or other snacks, as had been the case since its introduction in the 17th century. Over time, the rich tended to dine later and the usefulness of afternoon tea grew.

By the middle of the 19th century, it was established as a way for the upper classes, particularly women, to come together and socialise. It was less formal than a dinner and a good way to assess new people in a group. It also helped to fill a long gap between luncheon and dinner.

It quickly caught on, spreading down the social scale where it merged with working-class habits, in the shape of high tea: an early evening meal which often took the place of a more formal dinner. By the end of the century, afternoon tea was served in upper-class drawing rooms, middle-class hotels, and working-class tea rooms.

The first tea rooms opened in Glasgow in the 1870s, followed by several chains including Lyons and the ABC. Lockhart's Cocoa Houses also sold tea. They were very important in providing spaces where women could socialise without fear, and they helped to open up city centres as places for leisure as well as work.

Tea became a British national beverage during Queen Victoria's reign due to the expansion of tea plantations in India, which was then part of the British Empire. Lower taxes made tea more affordable for all levels of society to enjoy.

For the wealthy, afternoon tea evolved into an elaborate affair, an opportunity to parade one's wealth and social standing. Over time, people introduced decadent displays of cake stands, silver teapots, hand-stitched linens, and lace. This light meal became an important ceremony.

Ranger's House in Greenwich is a fine example of a place where afternoon tea would be a daily occasion. With its panelled parlours and collection of fine art, you can imagine the inhabitants of this Georgian villa enjoying a fine spread of delicious novelties. Today, afternoon tea remains a symbol of British refinement, a social occasion enjoyed by those who love decadence and formality.

Plain Scones

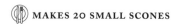

⏱ Preparation time 10 minutes   🕐 Cooking time 10–12 minutes

Scones and other cakes raised with baking powder have always been popular and are quick to make. There are two recipes that are similar to our modern scone: breakfast cakes and soda buns, both of which have a neutral dough that is excellent when buttered or eaten with jam. These use just a little sugar or none at all, where currants can be substituted instead for sweetness. Should you want to try this, add 115g of currants in the place of the sugar. Split the scones when cool and fill with clotted cream and English Heritage Raspberry Curd, or spread them with butter and English Heritage Blossom honey.

450g self-raising flour,
plus extra for dusting

115g cold unsalted butter, diced

pinch salt

60g caster sugar

175ml milk

1 tbsp lemon juice

SPECIAL EQUIPMENT:

a 4–5cm round pastry cutter

Preheat the oven to 200°C/gas mark 7 and get 2 baking trays ready.

Place the flour, butter, salt and sugar into a food processor and blend until the mixture is very fine and lump-free. Pour the mixture onto a work surface and make a well in the centre. Stir the milk and lemon juice together in a bowl or jug, then pour into the well in the dry ingredients.

Using a large fork, work steadily out from the centre to mix the flour quickly and gently into the liquid until you have an even mixture with no wet or dry patches. Scrape up any dough sticking to the work surface using a spatula and incorporate this into the mix. Do not knead the mixture. Simply pinch it together with your fingertips until it forms a ball. If it seems a little dry, add a splash more milk.

Scatter some flour over your work surface, rolling pin and baking trays. Gently roll the dough out to a thickness of 3cm on the floured work surface. Dip your cutter into some flour and then stamp out a round in the dough sheet and place it on the baking tray. Dipping your cutter in flour between each cut will ensure the scones rise evenly.

When you have used all the dough, dust the scones lightly with flour. Bake in the centre of the oven for 10–12 minutes, or until well risen and a light golden-brown. The scones are ready when they sound hollow when tapped on the bottom. Transfer the scones to a wire rack until completely cool, then store in an airtight tin or freeze.

Butterscotch Brownies

 MAKES 9

Preparation time 20 minutes

Cooking time 30 minutes

Rich, chewy, and buttery, these are the golden-hued cousin of the classic chocolate version. Instead of cocoa, these bars get their signature flavor from brown sugar and melted butter, creating a deep caramel-like taste with a soft, fudgy center and crisp edges. Often referred to as blondies, butterscotch brownies are a nostalgic treat that's simple to make but full of charm.

75g butter

175g soft light brown sugar

1 egg, beaten

50g chopped dates

75g flour

1 tsp baking powder

¼ tsp salt

1 tsp vanilla extract

SPECIAL EQUIPMENT:

a large shallow rectangular pan

Melt together the butter and soft brown sugar in pan, take off the heat, cool slightly, then add the egg and vanilla extract.

Mix the dry ingredients in a bowl, together with the dates and then pour in the butter and sugar mixture from the pan. Mix until combined and then pour into a large shallow rectangular pan so the mixture is about 5cm high.

Bake for 20-30 minutes.

Almond Macaroons

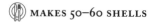 **MAKES 50–60 SHELLS**

*Preparation time 15 minutes
plus 20 minutes resting time*

Cooking time 15 minutes

You will get a smoother, glossier result if your almonds are ground as finely as possible and you dry them in a warm place for a couple of hours before using them. These macaroons are especially good spread with fresh raspberry jam.

140g ground almonds

200g icing sugar

seeds scraped from 2 vanilla pods

4 medium egg whites

pinch cream of tartar

60g caster sugar

FOR THE FILLING:

raspberry jam,
to sandwich

SPECIAL EQUIPMENT

a piping bag fitted with a
round nozzle

Before you begin, spread the ground almonds onto a baking sheet and leave them to dry in a warm place for 2 hours. Once they have dried, preheat oven to 140°C/gas mark 3. Line 2 baking sheets with non-stick baking paper.

Place the ground almonds, icing sugar and vanilla seeds into a food processor and blitz for 20 seconds to make the almonds as fine as possible and to combine them thoroughly with the sugar. Sift the mixture into a bowl.

Place the egg whites into the bowl of an electric mixer with the cream of tartar and beat on a medium speed until they become light and foamy. Increase the speed and add the caster sugar, a little at a time, until the sugar is fully incorporated and the mixture forms soft peaks.

Sift the almond mixture, one-third at a time, onto the egg whites, folding them together after each addition. Continue to fold until the mixture becomes smooth and glossy, then spoon into a piping bag fitted with a round nozzle and pipe rounds 2–3cm in diameter onto the prepared baking sheets, leaving 3cm between the rounds. Leave to rest for 20 minutes to allow a skin to form on top of the macaroons, then bake for 15 minutes until set.

Transfer the macaroons to a wire rack and leave to cool completely.

Use the raspberry jam to sandwich the macaroons together in pairs, and leave for 1 hour to allow the jam to soak in. The macaroons can be stored in an airtight container for up to 1 week, but they are best eaten after 24 hours.

Gingernuts

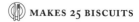 **MAKES 25 BISCUITS**

Preparation time 15 minutes

Cooking time 15–20 minutes

The spice mixture for these biscuits is lovely, with a little coriander being added for greater depth of flavour – an addition that is rarely seen today. The quantity of flour has been reduced to give a lighter, crisper result.

100g softened unsalted butter

75g caster sugar

20g black treacle or molasses

120g golden syrup

1½ tsp ground ginger

½ tsp ground allspice

½ tsp ground coriander

¾ tsp bicarbonate of soda

220g self-raising flour

100g demerara sugar

Preheat the oven to 180°C/gas mark 6. Line 2 baking sheets with non-stick baking paper.

Cream the butter and sugar in a large bowl until light and fluffy. Add the treacle or molasses and the syrup and beat the mixture until combined. In another bowl, sift all the ground spices, the bicarbonate of soda and the flour together then add to the butter mixture. Mix with your fingertips into an even dough that is free of lumps.

Pour the demerara sugar evenly onto a large flat dish. Now take a lump of dough about the size of a walnut, shape it into a ball and roll it in the demerara sugar, repeating with all the dough until the mixture is used up.

Arrange the balls at least 4cm apart on the prepared baking sheets and flatten each one slightly using a fork.

Bake for 5 minutes then turn the heat down to 160°C/gas mark 4 for a further 10–15 minutes.

The biscuits will rise and then fall. Once the surface of the biscuits cracks and they are firm and a dark golden brown all over remove them from the oven and leave them to cool for 10 minutes. Transfer the biscuits to a wire rack to cool completely and then store in an airtight container.

Shortbread

🕐 Preparation time 10 minutes plus 30 minutes chilling time

🍳 Cooking time 50 minutes

These are simply the finest biscuits to accompany the creamy puddings and fruit desserts found in this book, though it would be highly satisfying to enjoy one or two with nothing more than a cup of afternoon tea.

250g unsalted butter, diced

120g caster sugar, plus
1 tbsp for dredging

90g fine semolina

370g sifted plain flour

SPECIAL EQUIPMENT:
a 20cm square baking tin

Beat the butter until it is soft, and then add the sugar, semolina and flour. Knead lightly to combine. Press the dough evenly into the tin then chill for 30 minutes.

Just before you are ready to bake preheat the oven to 150°C/gas mark 3. Place the shortbread in the centre of the oven for 50 minutes, or until it is an even pale golden-brown colour. Remove from the oven and dredge with the tablespoon of caster sugar. Leave to cool for 10 minutes in the tin, then cut into fingers. When it is completely cold, lift the biscuits out of the tin and place them in an airtight container. These will keep for up to 1 week.

Tiffin

 MAKES 8

⏲ *Preparation time 15 minutes*

🍳 *Cooking time 2 hours*

The term 'tiffin' originally referred to a light midday meal or snack, a custom adopted from British colonial times. Over the years, it became associated with a no-bake, chocolatey treat, typically made with crushed biscuits, dried fruits, and a rich layer of chocolate. Popular in tea rooms and school lunchboxes, Tiffin cake became an easy and satisfying dessert that didn't require an oven.

120g unsalted butter

2 tbsp golden caster sugar

20g cocoa powder

3 tbsp golden syrup

225g digestive biscuits

225g dark or milk chocolate

25g raisins

25g glacé cherries

SPECIAL EQUIPMENT:

a small square or round baking tin

Place the butter, sugar, cocoa powder and golden syrup in a saucepan and heat and stir until the butter is melted and everything has combined.

Chop the biscuits into small pieces and slice the cherries into halves. Mix together and combine with the raisins. Gently drop everything into the melted mixture in the saucepan and give it all a good stir until combined.

Lightly grease a small square or round baking tin with a little softened butter and pour in the saucepan mixture. Use a spoon or your hand to press the mixture down to form the base.

In a separate bowl, gently melt the dark or milk chocolate (you can use a mixture of the two if you prefer) over a saucepan of boiling water. Do not allow steam to get into the chocolate or it will go lumpy. Pour the melted chocolate over the top of the biscuit mixture in the baking tin.

Place the Tiffin in the fridge to chill for at least 2 hours. Cut into bars and store in the fridge to keep fresh for up to 5 days.

AUDLEY END AND AVIS CROCOMBE

Audley End House is considered one of England's finest Jacobean mansions and was the family seat of the Barons Braybrooke.

Avis Crocombe entered domestic service at the age of thirteen, working as a servant in her brother's farmhouse in Devon. Avis later moved to Langley Hall in Norfolk, where she ran a staff that included kitchen maids, housemaids, and laundry maids. The national census of 1881 shows that Avis Crocombe was forty-three years old and working as the cook at Audley End. It would have been cheaper to employ Avis rather than a male chef, as she would have earned roughly half the wage of her male counterparts; nevertheless, she was at the top of her profession and could command a decent wage for a woman in the Victorian era.

Avis would have divided her time between Lord Braybrooke's London townhouse and the country estate at Audley End, as well as travelling with the family. In her role, Avis would have cooked for the Braybrookes and any other guests they would be entertaining, as well as their guests' entourage and the household's twenty-five service staff, above and below stairs. The kitchen workers would have prepared four different meals, four times a day, running an efficient operation that would begin at around six in the morning until late into the night.

In 2008, a multi-million-pound project was launched to create a living museum within the service wing of Audley End. A team of costumed interpreters were given the real-life roles of Avis and her team of staff, cooking and talking to visiting members of the public about life in service. It was through this real-life portrayal of Avis that a member of the public, Robert Stride, contacted the English Heritage to say he had Avis Crocombe's handwritten cookbook. The discovery of this personal manuscript provides a comprehensive account of Avis's cookery, adaptations, and important recipes collected over the entirety of her career. Most chefs would have kept a book of recipes, but finding an artifact of this quality added a significant layer of historical detail to the living museum at Audley End. Reading and recreating Avis's recipes gives you a deeper understanding of life in a Victorian kitchen.

Records show that Avis left the household in 1884 to marry Benjamin Stride, a widower with children, and she died in 1927 at the age of eighty-eight.

Queen Drop Biscuits

 MAKES 24

🕐 *Preparation time 10 minutes*

🍳 *Cooking time 10 minutes*

The recipe for these biscuits was found in Audley End cook Mrs Crocombe's very own book and has been updated for modern biscuit bakers by food historian Annie Grey. She comments that these biscuits are 'excellent indeed, and most moreish. They have the texture of cookies, with a cake-like middle and a biscuit-like exterior.'

225g butter

225g sugar

3 eggs

340g flour

225g currants

A few drops of almond extract

Preheat the oven to 180°C/gas mark 6. Cream the butter and add the sugar. Mix well, before sifting in the flour and adding the eggs. Mix until light and fluffy and tip in the currants and almond extract.

Using your hand or a tablespoon, drop equal quantities of the mixture onto a greased baking sheet. Don't put them too close together as the mixture will settle and expand outwards – you'll end up with a cross between a cookie and a cake.

Bake for about 10 minutes or until firm to the touch, and cool on a rack.

Banana Bread

SERVES 8

Preparation time 10 minutes

Cooking time 60 minutes

75g butter, plus extra for greasing

300g plain flour

pinch salt

1 tsp bicarbonate of soda

100g granulated sugar

3 eggs, beaten

3 ripe bananas

1 tbsp lemon juice

SPECIAL EQUIPMENT

a 23 x 13 x 7.5cm loaf tin

Grease a 23 x 13 x 7.5cm loaf tin. Preheat the oven to 190°C/gas mark 6. Sift the flour, salt and bicarbonate of soda together.

Cream the butter and sugar in a bowl. Beat in the eggs. Mash the bananas with the lemon juice. Add the bananas to the creamed mixture, then work in the dry ingredients. Put the mixture into the prepared loaf tin.

Bake for 50-60 minutes, until golden brown. Cool on a wire rack.

Bara Brith

 SERVES 6–8

🕐 *Preparation time 25 minutes plus overnight soaking*

🍳 *Cooking time 50–55 minutes*

'Plum breads', like this one, were, and are still, common and the recipes are almost impossible to distinguish from one another. Tea is used to moisten the fruit, and the resulting mixture requires no butter – a cake for hard times, you might think, but one that is delicious and healthy too. You can use any combination of tea and dried fruit, keeping the quantities the same.

400ml freshly made jasmine tea

350g dried dates

80g soft brown sugar

softened butter, for greasing

350g plain white flour

2 tsp baking powder

1 large egg, lightly beaten

25g flaked almonds

SPECIAL EQUIPMENT:

a 1kg loaf tin

The day before you bake, make the jasmine tea. Place the dates in a large bowl and strain the tea over them. Stir in the sugar, cover and leave overnight.

When you are ready to bake, preheat the oven to 180°C/gas mark 6. Grease the loaf tin with a little soft butter and line the base with a strip of non-stick baking paper.

Sift the flour and baking powder together into a bowl. Mix the beaten egg into the soaked dates then fold them into the flour mixture using a large metal spoon, working quickly but gently.

Transfer the batter to the loaf tin, smooth the surface and then scatter over the flaked almonds.

Set the loaf onto a baking tray and place in the centre of the oven for 50–55 minutes, turning the tin around after 30 minutes. The loaf is ready when a thin skewer pushed into the centre comes out clean, or a temperature probe registers 95°C. Remove from the oven and cool in the tin for 10 minutes. Transfer the cake to a wire rack to cool completely before storing in an airtight container. Serve in slices spread with butter and some English Heritage Blossom Honey.

Dark Gingerbread

 SERVES 6–8

Preparation time 20 minutes

Cooking time 45 minutes

This is a classic gingerbread, dark and moist. The quantity of flour is reduced here to make a lighter cake and there is added fresh root ginger to add spice and aroma. It can be iced or left plain and will keep for a week or more, after which it is best sliced and eaten spread with a little salted butter.

115g unsalted butter or lard, plus extra for greasing

225g black treacle

225g golden syrup

115g brown sugar, sieved if lumpy

50g finely grated fresh root ginger

375g plain flour

4 tsp ground ginger

4 tsp cinnamon

4 tsp mixed spice

pinch salt

1 tsp bicarbonate of soda

¼ pint milk

3 medium eggs

FOR THE ICING:

150g icing sugar

2 tbsp ginger wine or syrup

2 lobes of stem ginger in syrup, drained and finely chopped, to decorate

SPECIAL EQUIPMENT:

a 23cm square baking tin

Preheat the oven to 180°C/gas mark 6. Grease the baking tin and line the base with non-stick baking paper.

Place the treacle, syrup, sugar and butter or lard in a medium-sized saucepan over a low heat and warm until the fat has just melted. Remove from the heat and stir in the grated root ginger.

Sift the flour, spices, salt and bicarbonate of soda together into a large bowl until well blended then add the melted ingredients stirring well to combine. Lightly beat the milk and eggs together and then pour them into the treacle and flour mixture and stir to form a smooth, loose batter.

Pour the batter into the prepared tin and bake in the centre of the oven for 45 minutes, or until the gingerbread is evenly cooked and firm to the touch. Leave to cool in the tin on a wire rack for 15 minutes.

Make the icing by placing the icing sugar in a bowl and adding the ginger wine or syrup and mixing until you have a thick, pouring consistency. Turn the cooled gingerbread out of the tin, drizzle over the icing and sprinkle with the chopped ginger. Leave the icing to dry for 2–3 hours before serving. You can also transfer the gingerbread to an airtight container, but eat within 1 week of making.

Puddings

Plum Crumble

 SERVES 4

🕐 *Preparation time 15 minutes*

🍳 *Cooking time 45 minutes*

Although the fruit crumble as we know it today is most likely of twentieth-century origin, some historical recipes suggest scattering breadcrumbs over fruit puddings as an economical alternative to pastry. The recipe below is for a modern crumble topping: light, crisp and perfect for plums – or other fruits such as gooseberries or apples. Just vary the amount of sugar you use, remembering that the fruit will taste slightly sweeter once it's hot.

700g ripe plums, stoned
and quartered

50g caster sugar, to taste

FOR THE CRUMBLE TOPPING:
125g self-raising flour

50g ground almonds

100g unsalted butter

80g caster sugar

SPECIAL EQUIPMENT:
a 23 x 17cm baking dish

Preheat the oven to 180°C/gas mark 6.

Put the quartered plums into the baking dish, add the sugar and toss to coat. Taste a piece for sweetness and add a little more sugar if required.

Make the crumble topping by placing the flour, almonds, butter and sugar in the bowl of a food processor. Blend until the mixture resembles fine breadcrumbs then pulse the machine until the mixture begins to come together a little. Alternatively, grate the butter into the flour in a large bowl and rub in with your fingers, then add the almonds and sugar.

Spread the crumble evenly over the plums, then lightly smooth the surface. Place the dish on a baking tray to catch any drips and transfer to the oven.

Bake the crumble for 15 minutes, then reduce the heat to 160°C/gas mark 4, and continue cooking for another 30 minutes until the top is golden and the mixture is bubbling. Serve with custard (see page 116) or Jersey cream.

Cabinet Pudding

Preparation time 20 minutes

Cooking time 1 hour

In Georgian times, desserts were a real treat and a popular one was cabinet pudding, which was sometimes also known as chancellor's pudding. It's a traditional bread-and-butter pudding that was made with dried fruits and served with custard, a bit like many of the puddings we still eat today.

Butter, for greasing	1 pint milk
60g raisins	85g Sugar
A few thin slices bread and butter with the crusts cut off	¼ nutmeg
3 eggs	

Butter a pudding basin and line with a layer of raisins, then nearly fill the basin with the slices of bread and butter.

In another bowl, beat the eggs and add in the milk, sugar and grated nutmeg.

Mix well and pour onto the bread. Leave to stand for 30 minutes, then tie a floured cloth over the basin and boil for 1 hour.

Serve with custard.

Eve's Pudding

 SERVES 4

Preparation time 25 minutes

Cooking time 35 minutes

Eve's Pudding is a classic British dessert that pairs soft, sweetened apples with a light, buttery sponge topping. Thought to be named after the biblical Eve and her famous apple, this recipe is simple, wholesome, and full of cozy charm. Best served warm with a generous pour of custard or cream.

FOR THE FILLING:

2 large cooking apples (about 500g in total)

1 tbsp lemon juice

20g butter

2 tbsp caster sugar

FOR THE TOPPING:

75g butter

100g caster sugar

100g self-raising flour

2 free-range eggs, lightly beaten

1 tbsp boiling water

TO SERVE:

cream or custard

SPECIAL EQUIPMENT:

a 900ml capacity ceramic gratin dish, about 5cm deep

Preheat the oven to 180°C/gas mark 6.

Peel, core and roughly chop the apples. Add the apples to a saucepan with the lemon juice and 2 tablespoons of water. Stir, cover and cook briskly for five minutes until the apples are soft.

Add the butter and caster sugar and stir. Then transfer to a 900ml capacity ceramic gratin dish, about 5cm deep. Leave to cool while you prepare the topping.

For the topping, cream together the butter and caster sugar until fluffy and light.

Fold the flour and egg in alternate spoonfuls into the sugar mixture until blended, being careful to keep folding rather than stirring energetically – this will keep air in the mixture. Add a spoonful of boiling water to the mix.

Spoon the mixture over the apples. Cook in the oven for 30–35 minutes or until the topping is puffy and golden. Serve with cream or custard.

Christmas Pudding

MAKES 3 X 500G PUDDINGS

Preparation time 1 hour

Cooking time 4 hours initial steaming, then 3 hours to reheat

This recipe takes the best elements from several recipes for plum and other Christmas puddings. Only a small amount of egg is used to bind the mixture, resulting in a lighter, fruitier pudding – but it is essential to use high-quality dried fruit.

---

butter, for greasing

170g extra-large Muscatel (Lexia) raisins

170g currants

170g sultanas

115g dark muscovado sugar

1 tbsp black treacle

225g white breadcrumbs

2 medium eggs

170g grated suet

50g chopped candied peel

zest of ½ lemon, finely grated

¼ tsp freshly grated nutmeg

¼ tsp ground cinnamon

100ml Jubilee Stout or milk, to mix

few drops almond extract

SPECIAL EQUIPMENT:

3 x 500ml pudding basins

a pastry cutter or muffin ring

Butter the pudding basins well. Mix all of the rest of the ingredients together in a large bowl ensuring that everything is well blended.

Divide the mixture between the 3 basins.

Take 3 pieces of greaseproof paper and make a pleat down the centre of each to allow room for expansion during steaming. Cover the top of each pudding with a pleated piece of greaseproof paper followed by a pleated piece of foil and secure by tying kitchen string around the edge of the basin, leaving some extra string to make a handle for lifting the pudding.

If you have a large steamer, steam all of the puddings at once, ensuring that the steamer does not boil dry. Alternatively, steam each pudding in turn, keeping them in the fridge until you are ready to cook them.

If you do not have a steamer, fill the kettle with water and bring to the boil. Place a pastry cutter or muffin ring in the base of a 4-litre pan and put it on the hob. Set 1 of the 3 pudding basins on the ring in the bottom of the pan (this ensures that the basin does not crack) and add boiling water to a depth of 15cm. Turn the heat under the pan to medium and bring the water to a simmer. Continue simmering over low heat for 4 hours, topping up with boiling water as necessary. Steam each pudding in turn.

When the puddings are cold, wrap them in foil and store in a cool dark place for up to 1 year.

Baked Rice Pudding

 SERVES 4

⏱ Preparation time 5 minutes

🍲 Cooking time 3 hours including resting time

This baked version of a rice pudding is fuss-free and can even cook alongside your roast if you have more than one oven. The key to making a good rice pudding is in allowing plenty of time for the rice to cook – and you will note that this dish can seem very liquid up until the final third of the cooking time, when the rice begins to swell.

500ml whole milk
(Jersey for preference)

30g caster sugar

15g unsalted butter

50g pudding rice

1 bay leaf (optional)

nutmeg, freshly grated to taste

SPECIAL EQUIPMENT:

a 17cm square baking dish,
3–4cm deep

Preheat the oven to 140°C/gas mark 3.

Place the milk and sugar in a saucepan over a medium heat. Add the butter and stir until the milk is hot and the butter has melted.

Put the rice into the baking dish. Pour over the heated milk mixture, add the bay leaf, if using, and stir well.

Bake for 2½ hours, giving the pudding a stir about every 30 minutes.

Remove from oven and grate a little nutmeg over top. Turn oven up to 160°C/gas mark 4, and return the pudding to the oven for 15 minutes.

Remove the bay leaf, if using, and leave the finished pudding to rest in a warm place for 10 minutes. Serve with warmed jam or bottled fruits.

Trifle

⏱ Preparation time 1 hour 45 minutes split over 3 days

If one dessert sums up the British kitchen, it would probably be the trifle. This recipe is a combination of elements from several recipes. At a pinch, you can use puréed fresh raspberries to make up the jelly quantities – just sweeten to taste.

---

lemon sponge (see page 52)

600ml strawberry jelly
(see page 126)

3 tbsp homemade or sharp raspberry jam

100ml sweet sherry, or more,
to taste

1 quantity everyday custard
(see page 116)

FOR THE TOPPING:

600ml double cream

15g caster sugar

finely grated zest of 1 lemon

45ml Amontillado sherry

SPECIAL EQUIPMENT:

a large, attractive glass
serving bowl

Make the sponge and begin the jelly on the first day, leaving the jelly to drip overnight.

Cut the lemon sponge in half and spread the bottom half with the raspberry jam. Replace the top half and cut the sponge into small rectangles. Take a large glass serving bowl and line it with the sponge rectangles.

Sprinkle the sponge all over with the sherry, then finish the raspberry jelly and pour it over the sponge. Cover with cling film and chill overnight.

On the third day make the custard and set it aside to cool. Remove the trifle bowl from the fridge and peel back the cling film. Pour the custard over the raspberry jelly and smooth the surface with a palette knife. Re-cover with the cling film and store in a cool place until needed.

When you are ready to serve the trifle, remove the cling film and top with the topping. Whip the cream with the sugar, lemon zest and sherry until it forms soft peaks, then pile it on top of the custard, spreading it carefully to the edges of the dish.

Everyday Custard

 SERVES 6

Preparation time 5 minutes

Cooking time 30 minutes including 15 minutes infusing time

This quick recipe uses cornflour to thicken the sauce. It is an economical way of making custard and is perfect for a trifle (see page 114).

---

1 tbsp cornflour

450ml whole or Jersey milk

80g caster sugar

1 vanilla pod, split lengthways

4 large egg yolks

SPECIAL EQUIPMENT:

a heatproof glass bowl

a temperature probe

In a medium-sized bowl, mix the cornflour and just enough milk to make a thin paste. Set this aside and place the remaining milk, half the sugar and the vanilla pod in a pan. Slowly bring to the boil, whisking often to prevent sticking. Once it has boiled, remove the pan from the heat, cover with a lid and leave for 15 minutes to infuse.

Meanwhile, place the eggs yolks and the remaining sugar in a heatproof glass bowl and whisk until pale and fluffy.

Now remove the vanilla pod from the milk and scrape the seeds from the pod back into the pan. Place the pan over a medium heat. When

the mixture is simmering, pour
it onto the cornflour mixture
in the bowl, stir, and then pour
it back into the pan. Simmer
for 2–3 minutes, still stirring, to
cook the custard. If the custard
still tastes floury at this point,
continue cooking on a low heat
for another 1–2 minutes.

Beat the egg yolk mixture
once more and then pour the
simmering custard onto it,
whisking constantly to combine.

Rinse out the milk pan and half
fill with hot water. Place over a medium heat and set the bowl of
custard mixture on top, making sure that base of the bowl doesn't
touch the water. Cook, stirring continuously, until the custard
thickens. If you like, test with a temperature probe as you stir. The
custard needs to cook to 80–83°C to thicken. If you notice it curdling
at the bottom of the bowl, remove from the heat immediately.

Strain the cooked custard through a sieve into a serving jug or a cold,
clean bowl to stop it cooking any further. Either serve immediately or,
if using for a trifle, cool the custard, cover with cling film and store in
the fridge for up to 3 days.

Strawberry Jelly

 SERVES 4

⏱ Preparation time 20 minutes plus dripping overnight

⏱ Chilling time overnight

This delightful jelly has a beautiful colour and flavour. Do not be put off by the quantity of strawberries needed, because the pulp can be used in making strawberry water ice. The two dishes make a winning combination and would make a highly refreshing dessert to follow a summer lunch.

2kg ripe strawberries, hulled

110g plus 1–2 tsp caster sugar

clear apple juice

1 tsp lemon juice

approx 4 leaves gelatine

SPECIAL EQUIPMENT:

a square of muslin

a 500ml jelly mould

Place the strawberries in a large stainless steel or ceramic bowl, add 110g of caster sugar and mix together. Crush with a potato masher to form a fairly smooth mass.

Leave the berries and sugar to steep for 1 hour then transfer to a jelly bag (or a piece of muslin placed in a sieve) set over a large bowl. Do not press on the fruit or the juice will not be clear. Cover with a clean cloth, and leave in a cool place overnight to allow the strawberry juice to drip through the fabric into the bowl.

This amount of strawberries should yield approximately 500ml of juice. If it does not make enough, make up to 500ml with clear apple juice. If you have more than 500ml, you may need to use more gelatine. Stir the lemon juice into the strawberry juice and then add 1–2 teaspoons of caster sugar to taste, stirring to dissolve.

Place the sheets of gelatine into a bowl of cold water and leave to soak for 10 minutes. (If you prefer to serve the jelly in individual glasses, and do not intend to turn it out, you can use just 3 leaves of gelatine per 500ml of juice instead of 4.) Pour half of the strawberry juice into a small pan over a low heat. When the juice is hand hot remove it from the heat. Squeeze the gelatine sheets to remove excess water and add them to the warm juice, stirring to dissolve. Pour the juice and gelatine mixture into the bowl with the rest of the strawberry juice and stir to mix well.

Strain the mixture through a fine sieve into the mould and chill overnight to set. Turn the jelly out by dipping the mould in boiling water for a few seconds to loosen the edges.

COOKING
WITH ASPIC

In the Middle Ages, cooks discovered that if they simmered meat bones for long enough, the cooling broth would gel. Aspic is essentially a savoury jelly made from meat stock or broth that's been chilled until it sets.

It was a famous French chef, Marie Antoine Carême (1784–1833), who used aspic as a means to preserve food and elevated it into a way to decorate cold dishes. Aspic offered the chance to display dishes as not merely food, but spectacle. Sliced meats and vegetables, boiled eggs, seafood and shellfish were moulded into intricate shapes using copper or ceramic moulds. These delicacies would also have to be kept very cold to set properly, proving you must have access to ice, which was a valuable commodity.

As the hosts of refined dinner parties, the Victorians relished the opportunity to impress guests with their sophisticated presentation of food. Most of these ideas fell under the term 'service à la russe', a Russian-inspired way of presenting food from starters to dessert, one course at a time, usually at an elaborately decorated table. Glistening jellied creations would be the chilled, shimmering centrepiece of a formal dinner, adding visual drama and a demonstration of a chef's culinary expertise.

In the kitchens of Brodsworth Hall in South Yorkshire, you can imagine the busy behind-the-scenes world of Victorian cookery and housekeeping. Their remarkable collection of moulds offers incredible insight into the care and creativity needed to prepare complex and ornamental dishes. The shapes range from simple domes to intricate fluted designs.

In Britain, times have changed; we are now much more familiar with sweet, fruit-flavoured jellies. Not many households in Britain would have a savoury aspic centrepiece at the dinner table, but in some parts of the world, traditional menus still have a little room on their table for aspic delicacies and delights.

French terrines are similar to pâté, cooked with any combination of rich game meat or vegetables high in pectin, baked in terrine moulds and served cold. Kholodets are enjoyed in Ukraine, Russia and parts of Eastern Europe. These savoury jellies are made by boiling cheap cuts of meat and bones and then left to gel naturally. The more sophisticated galantine or stalivnoye is set with clarified gelatine and can be made with cuts of meat, fish or vegetables and can feature intricately carved boiled eggs and be decorated with caviar.

Chocolate Soufflé

 SERVES 4 PEOPLE

Preparation time 20 minutes

Cooking time 10 minutes

This lovely soufflé is a perfect dinner-party dessert. The flour has been removed from the original recipe because it is not really necessary; without it, this dish has the advantage of being gluten-free. It is delicious served with vanilla ice cream.

TO LINE THE RAMEKINS:

softened butter, for greasing

1 tsp cocoa powder

1 tsp caster sugar

FOR THE SOUFFLÉ:

80g plain chocolate (65–72% minimum cocoa solids)

3 medium eggs

1½ tbsp caster sugar

1 tbsp brandy (optional)

SPECIAL EQUIPMENT:

4 x 120ml ramekins

a large heatproof bowl

a roasting tin

Preheat the oven to 200°C/gas mark 7.

Butter the ramekins well, taking care to ensure the top edge is buttered to allow the soufflé to rise without sticking. Combine the cocoa powder and sugar together and sprinkle a little of the mixture into each ramekin, rolling it around until the insides are coated. Set the ramekins aside until needed.

Break up the chocolate and place it in a large heatproof bowl set over a pan of barely simmering water, making sure that the bottom of the bowl does not touch the water. Do not stir vigorously, but stir occasionally to make sure that the chocolate does not seize on the bottom of the bowl and go stiff.

Place the eggs and sugar in the bowl of an electric mixer and beat until the mixture is mousse-like and very pale and thick. Alternatively, whisk with an electric hand whisk.

When the chocolate has fully melted, remove it from the heat and fold in one-third of the egg mixture. Then, working quickly and carefully, fold in the remaining egg mixture, along with the brandy, if liked.

Divide the mixture between the ramekins, wiping off any spills. Place them in a roasting tin and add enough boiling water to reach halfway up the sides of the ramekins.

Place in the oven for 10 minutes until risen but still a little soft in the middle and serve immediately.

Cherry Clafoutis

 SERVES 4

⏱ *Preparation time 15 minutes plus 30 minutes resting time*

🍳 *Cooking time 20–25 minutes plus 10 minutes cooling time*

A clafoutis, or batter pudding, can be made with any tart fruit, but cherries are the classic. Some recipes used currants in winter, but recommended damsons, plums, apricots or gooseberries in season – showing just how flexible this dish can be. The stones of the cherries are left in here because they impart a subtle almond flavour to the finished clafoutis. Warn your guests to go gently, though, because they will encounter stones in the pudding.

400g ripe cherries, stems removed

80g caster sugar

2 large eggs

200ml milk

100g plain flour

pinch salt

5g unsalted butter

icing sugar, for dusting

SPECIAL EQUIPMENT:
a 25cm ovenproof frying pan

Place the cherries in a bowl with 40g of the sugar, stir to mix and set aside.

Place the eggs in another bowl and whisk for a minute or two until frothy. Add the milk and whisk again to combine. Sift the flour, salt and remaining 40g of sugar into a third bowl and make a well in the centre. Pour in the egg and milk mixture and whisk to combine into a smooth batter. Set aside to rest for half an hour.

Preheat the oven to 180°C/gas mark 6.

Heat a 25cm ovenproof frying pan over a medium heat and add the butter. When it begins to foam, add the cherries and any juice to the pan.

Give the batter a stir to fold any foam that has settled on top back into the mixture and pour carefully into the pan. Place into the oven for 20–25 minutes, or until set and golden on top. Allow the clafoutis to cool for 10 minutes before dusting with icing sugar and serving.

Spotted Dick

 SERVES 6–8

🕐 *Preparation time 20 minutes*

🍳 *Cooking time 2 hours*

This is a classic steamed pudding that's made with suet instead of butter. The 'spotted' name comes from currants within the sponge the 'Dick' seems to come from the shortened Old English names for pudding: *puddog* or *puddick*.

300g self-raising flour

1 tsp baking powder

150g suet (fresh or packet)

75g caster sugar

100g currants

zest 2 lemons

275–300ml milk

butter, for greasing

SPECIAL EQUIPMENT:

a 2 pint pudding basin

In a bowl, mix together the flour, baking powder, suet, sugar, currants and lemon zest. Add the milk, mixing slowly until all is incorporated. You're looking for a mixture of dropping consistency.

Liberally butter a 2 pint pudding basin and spoon in the mixture. Cover with a lid. It's easiest to buy a plastic basin with a fitted lid. If you're using a glass or porcelain basin, make a lid from a double sheet of pleated foil and secure with string. It is worth making a foil or string handle for the pudding so that you can get the basin out of the steamer safely.

Place in a steamer and steam for 2 hours. Make sure there's a good brisk boil for the first 20 minutes and then turn the heat down to medium-low. If you don't have a steamer, simply place an upturned saucer in the base of a deep saucepan and pour over boiling water straight from the kettle. Gingerly place in the pudding.

Turn out the pudding onto a serving plate and serve immediately with plenty of custard.

OSBORNE HOUSE

In 1845, Queen Victoria and Prince Albert bought Osborne House as a country retreat for their growing family. Albert redesigned Osborne after deciding to demolish the original estate house, and then completed the project with Thomas Cubitt, a prominent London architect. With its Italianate towers, grandiose portico, and Corinthian columns, the Osborne style became hugely influential in Victorian architecture.

With over three hundred and fifty acres, the estate includes a private beach, parkland, formal gardens, and terraces. The walled garden has been restored to its late Victorian use, growing an array of cut flowers and espaliered fruit trees.

Food has always been an essential part of family life, but it was a symbol of status during Victorian times. The Queen's kitchens were staffed by dozens of people who produced vast amounts of food for the daily consumption of the monarch, her family, and any visiting dignitaries, as well as their entourage of staff and servants. Victorians introduced the concept of three-course meals and placed immense importance on sequential service. The kitchen staff also had their own hierarchy and ate accordingly, with varying degrees of privilege according to their position in the household.

Afternoon tea became a fashionable event during Queen Victoria's reign. Most cakes contained fruit, nuts, or seeds, and children were forbidden to consume them for fear of choking. As a suitable alternative, a plain sponge with a layer of jam was introduced and named the Victoria Sponge. Battenberg cake was named in honour of the marriage of the Queen's granddaughter, Princess Victoria, to Prince Louis of Battenberg in 1884. Another Victorian creation, Osborne pudding, is a derivative of traditional bread and butter pudding, made using brown bread and marmalade and a cream-based custard.

Osborne House gives a unique view of Queen Victoria and Prince Albert's private life and the importance of time spent together as a family. The delightful Royal Swiss Cottage was built as a "royal playhouse" for the young Princes and Princesses. Each child grew flowers, fruit, and vegetables to sell to Prince Albert. Everything in the cottage kitchen is in three-quarter scale, which made it easier for the children to bake pies, cakes, and pastries to serve to the family for afternoon tea. In the Queen's room, the full-size dining table is laid ready for afternoon tea, commemorating the 12th of July 1861, the last time the royal family were all together in the cottage.

Osborne Pudding or Bread & Butter Pudding

 SERVES 6

Preparation time 20 minutes plus 30 minutes soaking time

Cooking time 50 minutes plus 5 minutes resting time

Original recipes recommended grated citrus peel for bread and butter pudding, but a spoonful or two of marmalade gives a sweeter zing that sets this dish off perfectly. You can vary the richness of the pudding by altering the ratio of cream to milk.

800ml mixed cream and milk, half of each

120g caster sugar

4 medium eggs

4 yolks

75g softened unsalted butter

300g stale sliced bread

75g English Heritage Blood Orange Marmalade (or other orange marmalade)

25g granulated sugar

SPECIAL EQUIPMENT:

a 20cm square ovenproof dish

a large roasting tin

Place the mixed cream and milk in a saucepan over a medium heat, add half the sugar and stir. Meanwhile, in a large bowl, beat the eggs and yolks with the remaining sugar until light and fluffy. When the milk mixture reaches simmering, pour it into the egg mixture and beat to amalgamate. Quickly strain it through a sieve into a large, cold bowl and set aside.

Butter the sliced bread and then spread with marmalade. Cut the slices in half and then arrange them overlapping in the ovenproof dish with the crusts uppermost.

Carefully pour the custard over the bread. Leave to stand for 30 minutes, or until all the liquid has been absorbed. Sprinkle over the granulated sugar.

Preheat the oven to 140°C/gas mark 3. Fill the kettle and bring to a boil. Place the ovenproof dish in a large roasting tin. Pour in enough boiling water to come halfway up the sides of the dish. Bake for 50 minutes, or until lightly set and golden brown.

Remove from the oven and let the pudding sit for 5 minutes to rest before serving.

Index

Conversions

WEIGHT CONVERSIONS		VOLUME CONVERSIONS	
Grams	Ounces	Millilitres	Fluid Ounces
10g	¼oz	50ml	2fl oz
15g	½oz	80ml	2¾fl oz
20g	¾oz	100ml	3½fl oz
30g	1oz	125ml	4fl oz
40g	1½oz	150ml	5¼fl oz
50g	1¾oz	175ml	6fl oz
60g	2¼oz	200ml	7fl oz
70g	2½oz	225ml	8fl oz
80g	2¾oz	250ml	9fl oz
90g	3¼oz	275ml	9½fl oz
100g	3½oz	300ml	10½fl oz
150g	5½oz	350ml	12fl oz
200g	7oz	400ml	14fl oz
250g	9oz	450ml	16fl oz
300g	10½oz	500ml	18fl oz
350g	12oz	750ml	26½fl oz
400g	14oz	1 litre	35fl oz
450g	1lb		
500g	1lb 2oz		

LIQUIDS

Spoons & Cups	Millilitres
½ teaspoon	2.5ml
1 teaspoon	5ml
1 tablespoon	15ml
¼ cup	60ml
⅓ cup	80ml
½ cup	125ml
1 cup	250ml

OVEN TEMPERATURES

Gas mark	Celsius	Fahrenheit
1	140°C	275°F
2	150°C	300°F
3	160°C	325°F
4	180°C	350°F
5	190°C	375°F
6	200°C	400°F
7	220°C	425°F
8	230°C	450°F
9	250°C	475°F
10	260°C	500°F

Credits

Senior Commissioning Editor
George Brooker

Writer
Emma Russell

Proofreader
Elise See Tai

Indexer
Ingrid Lock

Editorial Management
George Brooker
Jane Hughes
Charlie Panayiotou
Lucy Bilton
Patrice Nelson

Contracts
Rachel Monte
Ellie Bowker

Design
Nick Shah
Deborah Francois

Art Direction
Helen Ewing

Cover and Interior Design
Helen Ewing

Illustrator
Anastasiya Levashova

Finance
Nick Gibson
Jasdip Nandra
Sue Baker
Tom Costello

Inventory
Jo Jacobs
Dan Stevens

Production
Claire Keep
Katie Horrocks

Marketing
Louis Patel

Sales
David Murphy
Victoria Laws
Group Sales teams
across Digital, Field,
International and
Non-Trade

Operations
Group Sales
Operations team

Rights
Rebecca Folland
Tara Hiatt
Ben Fowler
Ruth Blakemore
Marie Henckel